The Day Job Survival Kit

For Writers, Artists, Crafters, and Anyone Else with a Dream

By Durga Walker

Day Job Survivor

Publishing services provided by **Archangel Ink**

ISBN: 1517342368
ISBN-13: 978-1517342364

To

Master Ram

Table of Contents

Introduction

My current day job as a newspaper reporter has taught me not to bury the lead, so here it is:

The Day Job Survival Kit is about staying creative even though you have a day job and then purposely applying the creative process to transform your job into a positive force in your art and your life.

A day job by definition is not a chosen profession or a career. A day job is something you do to earn money because you can't survive doing what you really want to do. There's nothing inherently evil about day jobs, although we do tend to blame them for everything, but the truth is that they can be enormous pains in the behind and enormously depressing, if we let them be.

Through years of holding every imaginable day job—from shoveling coke at an oil refinery to filing (and falling asleep) in a basement archive, and almost everything in between—I've learned a few things about surviving on the job and, along the way, thriving as a creative person. From one artistic day-jobber to another, I can promise you that there are no principles here that I do not practice myself to make my own life better.

I wrote this book specifically for artists and craftspeople because folks involved in creative pursuits often have a hard time of it on the job market and end up working in fields they have no interest in just to pay the rent. Forty hours a week at a pointless job makes it all but impossible to do the art the job is supposed to support. Life becomes a hamster wheel.

Yet we may never experiment with the principles that can help us escape this cycle because they are packaged for other audiences, such as entrepreneurs and top salesmen in the fast-paced moneymaking world. This is truly a shame because these principles are true for everyone with a dream of any kind.

Some years ago, I started studying these principles and took an extended course with a motivational teacher. Over the years, I've continued learning, and one thing I've learned is this: no matter who you are or what line of work you're in, the creative process, used with imagination, will help bridge the gap between where you are and where you want to be.

While we're on the subject, I would caution you against confusing imagination with creation. You cannot breathe without creating something. Every new moment is a new creation. This is something no one can escape. However, using our imaginations is a choice. You can choose to take part in each new moment with awareness and imagination, or you can plod along through your circumstances, bearing the great weight of your day job on your back.

It's no use denying that the world is getting harder to live in. Good luck doing everything you want to, no matter what anyone says. Things will certainly come your way that you won't be happy with, but you always have the choice of how to respond to any situation. This is your most basic freedom, and no one can take it away from you. The way you respond shapes your world. If you are not happy with your world, change the way you respond.

We'll start this book by looking at the creative process in its simplest form. These principles form the basis for the entire book and all the exercises. We'll move on to some suggestions about dealing with the day-jobbing artist's greatest complaints: no creative time and no creative space. After that, we'll look at surviving the day job while being creative, each aspect expressed in terms that relate to the process of making art. The final section focuses on using these principles in specific ways to escape the day job once and for all. Yes, Virginia, there is a Santa Claus.

While I can't promise you the moon and the stars, I can promise that if you unlock the potential of the creative process you're already using and apply it to the rest of your life, everything will change.

I: The Creative Process

Let's take a close look at the creative process and see how it actually works in our lives, not how we think it works. Let's suspend all the angst, doubts, and blocks. They are a sideshow, and not a very helpful one. Instead of focusing on all the ways we sabotage our art, let's look at the bare bones of how we get from idea to product. It's much simpler than you might have imagined.

If you look closely, you'll see that the first thing you do when starting a creative project is picture what you want. You might call this a spark of inspiration because it seems to have come like a bolt from the blue. Now you're all fired up and, almost without effort, your mind gets busy putting the puzzle pieces together, figuring out how to make this wonderful idea a reality.

You may not know how you'll get to the end, but you're certain you can accomplish at least the first steps. You decide to go for it. You assemble your tools and get to work.

Once you're working, all sorts of agonizing doubts and fears may arise, but again, we're not concerned with those here. This book is about grabbing those all-important first steps of the process—forming that image and acting on it. Happily, once you get comfortable with this simple two-fold process, you might find that you're no longer bothered by those doubts and fears.

To these two basic elements, I'm adding a third. Together, they form the basis of everything that follows in these pages.

Picture it.

Act on it.

Give thanks for it.

Let's unpack each of these ideas before we go on. And please don't skip over that third element. It's the most important of all.

Picture it

Forming an image in the mind is the most natural thing in the world, whether you're an artist or not. Every action we take is preceded by an image in the mind, even down to getting out of bed in the morning.

As human beings, we are born with this image-forming ability. As artists and craftspeople, we've become skilled in using it with creative intent. However, while many of us apply this ability to the artistic process with great success, we often struggle with accomplishing other important things in our lives.

It's my belief that these skills are transferrable and that, with some understanding of the creative process we're already engaged in, we can direct our minds toward solving the thorny problems that come along with being creative people with day jobs.

Just as forming an image of what you want to create in your artistic medium is the first step in making something, the first step to getting your day job in perspective is forming a clear image of what you want out of life in general. What is your vision or dream for yourself? Where are you going? Where do you want to go? Remember, your present day job is only a small part of who you are.

I'm using the word "vision" interchangeably with the word "dream." You most certainly have dreams, but I like to use the word vision because it makes me think of something you can actually see in your mind. It's not a fantasy. It's achievable because you can form an image of it and move toward accomplishing it.

At the same time, a vision is not a goal. Let's look at the difference.

A vision is much bigger and less specific than a goal. A goal needs to be measurable so you know when you've achieved it, while a vision is the big picture of who and what you are and what you'd like to accomplish. Goals are what you use to bring your vision into reality. Without a greater vision, it's very hard to set meaningful goals.

For example, as part of my own vision, I see myself putting out into the world ideas I feel are important and useful. As an artist, I envision doing this through the means of writing, letterpress printing, and book arts. This is a broad and nonspecific vision, so I've used the exercises at the end of this chapter to specify in greater detail what I see for myself, forming a detailed image of my vision that I can call to mind whenever I feel lost at sea. This vision has helped me set goals to accomplish it.

One of my first goals has been to get this book into your hands. To do this, I've had to set a series of smaller goals, such as writing it, publishing it, and marketing it. Each of these can be broken down into bite-size goals that are achievable and measurable and will bring me to the completion of my larger goal and eventually to living out my vision. Because they are so important, I focus more on setting goals in a later section of this book.

While goal setting may sound prosaic to some, it doesn't negate the creative dance I'm doing while writing this book. Believe me, there's quite a lot of dancing going on! But goals support both the dance and the ultimate vision. As markers along the way, they help me stay on track. I use them to measure how far I've come and to make sure I'm going in the right direction.

A vision, formulated as a clear image, functions as a lifeline. You can use it to direct the course of your life, as a captain steers a ship, or you can have no vision and be content to drift aimlessly, with no destination and no way to get there. It's your choice.

You may have so many unfulfilled dreams rattling around inside your head that you haven't got a clue where to start. You might not even want to try because it hurts. But do try. Make friends with your dreams. Use the exercises here to coax them out and crystallize them into one clear image.

To use the nautical analogy again, a vision functions much like the keel on a sailboat, cutting through the sea to keep the boat upright and moving forward. It isn't surprising that, without a vision, we have trouble dragging ourselves through our days.

I would urge you to create a vision that you can carry in your mind while you go about your work. Don't let the duties of your job affect the integrity of your vision. Let it exist in your mind, untouched by your present circumstance. It's like a song that carries you on and inspires your heart but that never changes, whether you hear it at a concert or in a hospital waiting room.

There is nothing mystical about this first, very crucial step. As Wallace Wattles wrote all the way back in 1907, "All you need is to know what you want and to want it badly enough so that it will stay in your thoughts."

It is precisely this skill that we apply to our art, but often fail to apply to our lives.

One more word about arriving at the image of your vision: you want it to be clear and steady once you have it, but don't be afraid to let it evolve as it is forming. This is, after all, the creative process. It may be that only a glimpse is clear at the start. Follow that glimpse, letting it morph into what is true for you. It will soon be so powerful you won't be able to resist it.

My own vision took me years to embrace. First, I had to shovel all the "shoulds" out of the way. I had a lot of crazy ideas about what I *should* want to do with my life. Then one day, I said, "Wait a minute! I don't care if no one understands this. It's my vision, and it's what I want." Immediately, things began to happen. Of course, I went from there through several more stages before arriving at what was true for me. That's life. But if I hadn't claimed what I saw, it wouldn't have been able to grow.

Your vision is your heart's desire. Give it the time and space it needs to become clear. And don't worry—it doesn't have to take you as long as it did me.

Before we go on, let's confront the elephant in the room: the Money Monster.

There's nothing in the world wrong with having money. As Dolly Parton said when she was introducing one of her making-the-best-of-poverty ballads, "So I wrote a song about it and it made me a lot of money. It's amazing how many problems money can solve."

I'm the last person to suggest you should live on air. I've been on both sides of that fence, and having money is my personal preference. Poor people sing the praises of poverty, but rich people don't. Rich people recognize that our society is set up in such a way that we need money to thrive. You deserve to thrive and you deserve to have money. It's why you took a day job in the first place.

As you let your vision form, I would encourage you to face any fears you might have concerning your financial future—especially if you're envisioning yourself stuck in a day job for the rest of your life. Divorce those fears from your vision. Set them aside and deal with them another time. You can include money in your vision or not, but don't let financial fear hinder your dreams.

In his book *The Success Principles,* Jack Canfield addresses a deep fear creative people seem to share. He writes, "What often stops people from expressing their true desire is they don't think they can make a living doing what they love to do."

Canfield describes celebrities who became, for example, talk show hosts because they loved to hang out and talk with people. If they felt fear, they didn't let it stop them. But you don't need to be a celebrity.

"My friend Diane Brause," he says, "who is an international tour guide, makes a living hanging out and talking with people in some of the most exciting and exotic locations in the world."

He cites a pro golfer who loves to golf and a comedian who likes to make people laugh, then writes, "My sister loves to design jewelry and hang out with teenagers. Donald Trump loves to make deals and build buildings. I love to read and share what I've learned with others in books, speeches, and workshops. It's possible to make a living doing what you love."

I've included one of Canfield's exercises below because I believe it's helpful in addressing these fears.

Form a clear image of your vision, whatever it may be, so that you can start to make it happen.

Thoughts and actions for

Picture it

1. Get the Money Monster out of the way.

Here's an exercise Canfield offers in *The Success Principles*. It might help free your mind of worries that could limit your vision. By the way, *The Success Principles* is a great book for further exploration.

Make a list, he says, of 20 things you love to do, then think of ways you could make a living doing some of those things.

"If you love sports," he says, "you could play sports, be a sportswriter or photographer, or work in sports management as an agent or in the front office of a professional team. You could be a coach, a manager, or a scout. You could be a broadcaster, a camera operator, or a team publicist. There are myriad ways to make money in any field you love."

If you do not have a comprehensive knowledge of your art or craft field, study it until you do. There's a place for you in it, whether it's making it or supporting it.

Once you know you don't have to worry about making money in your chosen field, you will feel freer to let your imagination soar when it comes to forming your vision.

2. Put ALL of it down on paper.

This exercise is to help you clarify all aspects of your greater vision. As you do this, remember that it's not the words that will carry you forward but the intent and purpose behind them.

Take some time to sit and write, or carry paper and pen with you and jot notes down while you work. Write down—by hand and from the heart—everything you want to do. Write pages and pages and pages. There are many ways you can do this. Some people recommend making lists, while others suggest descriptive paragraphs. Do whatever works for you, but it's better to have excess ideas than not enough.

Go back and extract the bits that are authentic, that feel right to you. Now write a true description of your heart's desire. It could be your ideal day, a word version of mental photographs of your life as you would like it to be, or a narrative of an ideal future moment. Write it in the present as if it's already happening.

If the present tense sounds like an odd recommendation, remember two things: First, your mind will begin to figure out ways to materialize anything you tell it is already happening (just look at how it strives to materialize your fears). And second, it *is* already happening because you just took the first step.

Act on it

Look once again at your artistic process and you'll probably see that you rarely if ever throw yourself into a project you don't believe you can do. What would be the sense in that? Even if the end goal seems impossible, you have to believe you can achieve the initial steps or why should you go for it?

"Going for it" is a wonderful way to think about taking action. It embodies passion and movement and desire and fun, but once we unpack it, we see it also contains belief, the secret ingredient in everything we do and the key to acting on our visions.

For many of us, believing in our visions is the hardest thing in the world. How is it possible to believe in something that's the opposite of what we see happening in our lives? But we must, because simply having a vision is not enough.

As Wattles writes, "Behind your clear vision must be the purpose to realize it, to bring it out in tangible expression. And behind this purpose must be an invincible and unwavering faith that the thing is already yours—that it is at hand and you only have to take possession of it."

This chapter is about developing the faith, or belief, you need to achieve your vision.

A day job can grow to the size of the Goodyear blimp in your mind and flatten you against the walls if you let it, to the point that the job seems to be more real than your dreams. Your day job is very real, but so are your dreams and desires. If you're going to embark on achieving your dream, you'll have to believe in it with such great force that your day job shrinks to its rightful size in your mind.

If you've done the work of creating your vision and forming a clear image of it, you can push back at the blimp with the strength of belief in yourself. Not only that, but you can create this belief in your mind and reinforce it every day.

Let's look at the nature of the beliefs we hold. People in general believe all sorts of crazy things for the craziest of reasons, but many of our unexamined beliefs come from simple repetition. We hear messages repeated over and over in advertising or TV shows, and we hear adages that have been handed down for generations. Although it's up to us to examine these messages and then confirm or disprove our belief in them, most often we don't. We carry them around in our minds and let them guide our actions.

Look at how you learned to spell. A word and its spelling was repeated over and over to you until your mind accepted it as truth, and now, if I told you CAT was spelled D-O-G, you wouldn't believe me. In this way, so many other ideas that may or may not be true have been repeated to us so many times that we accept them without question.

Many artists are proud of questioning what they think of as authority or status quo, pleased to see themselves functioning as the conscience of society, yet they fail to question some of the most basic guiding principles in their lives, such as why they might hold prosperity in contempt or equate poverty with artistic purity. It's beliefs like these that keep artists starving. If an artist has chosen this position with intent, more power to him. But it makes no sense for any artist, or any human being, to be subject to an undesired circumstance that is simply a result of unexamined beliefs.

Your present circumstance is the result of choices you've made in the past, and these choices have been based on your beliefs. Look around at your life and ask yourself how you got to where you are. Look at the beliefs you've based your decisions on. Do you like where you're living? Ask yourself why you choose to live there. If you follow this line of thought back far enough, you'll find the belief about yourself that this decision was based on. If you don't like your house, change your belief and make a different decision. Maybe you don't believe you deserve or can afford a different house. Challenge this belief. You don't have to let it shape your life.

It's true that sometimes our decisions are guided by circumstances beyond our control. I'm experiencing this very thing in my own life as I write this book. Until recently, my plans were to relocate to another country to be with family. I spent many years in that country and was overjoyed at finally being able to go home. But the situation on the world stage has shifted, and this country is now too dangerous to travel to. With great sadness, I decided to change my plans.

Such a world circumstance is beyond my control, but my response to the choice is not. There is always a free choice to be made at any given moment in time. In this case, I could choose to wallow in heartbreak or to pick myself up and go on in another way. I've chosen the latter. Some of the beliefs at play here are that I can be happy wherever I am, that I can create a rich and fulfilling life wherever I may be, and that God wants me to be prosperous, happy, and safe. If I chose to believe that the world was conspiring against me and I could never be happy unless I was where I wanted to be, my life would be a miserable affair indeed.

Take a look at the beliefs that are guiding your decisions and see if they're working for you or against you. Watch your thoughts throughout the day. If you find yourself repeating thoughts like, "I'll never get out of this job," "I must be a lousy artist," and "I'll always be broke," understand that these are habitual thoughts that only have the validity you give them. You can choose other beliefs about yourself that will work much more in your favor.

I'm not telling you what to believe. This is for you to arrive at yourself. But I am urging you to examine your beliefs very closely and make sure they're based on truths and values you are satisfied with. Many of the unexamined beliefs we hold bear no relation to the truth of the matter and are simply making life harder for us. In fact, you might be surprised to find your mind repeating mental messages that are in conflict with what you think you believe. This can only cause chaos in your life.

The affirmation exercise at the end of this chapter can help you create a list of new thoughts to repeat to yourself throughout the day. This exercise is meant to begin retraining your mind—your mental computer—to function the way you want it to. If you repeat often enough, "I am a great guitarist. I write excellent music that people love to listen to," you will begin to believe it and to make decisions based upon that belief, such as taking the time you need to practice, buying a better guitar, and playing in public. Eventually, these decisions can lead to things like writing music people love to listen to.

If you don't believe in the effectiveness of this idea, don't just dismiss it. Ask yourself why you don't believe in it. Follow that line of questioning all the way back to see where your skepticism began, and then decide what you really believe. Above all, give it a shot. You might be surprised.

Here's an idea to use if you really can't see past your present circumstances while you're developing your belief in yourself. One of the jobs of a novelist is to weave such a convincing fictional world that the reader suspends disbelief—in other words, the reader stops questioning whether this or that could actually happen and simply surrenders his imagination to the story. This could be a helpful concept for you.

Treat your vision like a story you're reading. Suspend your own disbelief. Keep your feet on the ground, of course, but train your mind to look past what you see as the reality of your present. Just as you would accept the fictional world of a beloved novel, focus on the "fictional" possibilities of your future.

This is not to be understood as an excuse to space out and shirk your current responsibilities. In fact, if you do shirk them, you'll never advance to your desired future. You have to learn to do both at once.

You already do this with your art when you look at the raw material and see the finished product. Now do the same thing with your vision. Go for it.

Thoughts and actions for
Act on it

1. Create the belief.

Fashion a list of affirmations from the stuff of your vision. Make sure every one reaffirms your belief in yourself. Phrase them in the positive, not the negative.

"I am creative and successful. My work is vibrant and dynamic and speaks to people's hearts. People love my work. My studio is thriving, and I am attracting more and more success every day."

Write affirmations that pull you up when you are down. Don't worry if you don't believe in them at first. Just write affirmations that you WANT to believe.

You are changing your thought habits. In time, your beliefs will come into alignment with them, and your actions will follow. At that point, you'll automatically begin doing things that will lead you in the direction of fulfilling your affirming thoughts.

2. Exercise your faith like a muscle.

Repeating affirmations is a good beginning, like limbering up stiff muscles. Now you can start building the strength of those muscles by noticing every time your circumstances fulfill your "affirmative" expectations. If you've been affirming to yourself that you're a good painter, make sure you acknowledge it the next time someone compliments your work. No more brushing off of compliments! They are telling you that your affirmations are working and you are changing into the you of your vision.

Feel your own strength and see how your belief is growing. Say your affirmations from this deeper place. Picture your faith strengthening. Use your creative power of visualization to see yourself change.

Give thanks for it

Nothing we make on the face of this earth is made by ourselves alone—not a decision, a work of art, or a loaf of bread. We are each part of the great creative force that made us, and nothing is made without the power of that force. Believing that we are creators in our own right is where many of us go off track.

Giving thanks for what we have is important, but giving thanks for what we do not yet have is just as important. When Wattles wrote that the faith behind our purpose must be invincible and unwavering, he was pointing to the kind of faith that knows it receives as soon as it asks. This is the point at which to first give thanks.

Gratitude is a surprising thing. On the one hand, it's something we offer God for all His blessings to us. It conveys our love and appreciation, our praise and acknowledgement of His gifts.

On the other hand, if we give thanks with all our hearts, we soon discover that gratitude itself is another gift from God because, while we're being grateful for what we've been given, the very act of being grateful benefits us in ways we can't count.

To start with, remembering to be grateful helps us stay open to all the positive things that come our way, and the fact is that we are being blessed at every moment. Think of the sun, our food, and the unclaimed opportunities that pop up while we're not looking. It's up to us to see them and receive them. A habit of giving thanks keeps us receptive and aware of blessings we might otherwise miss.

Nowhere is this more visible than in situations where we're not particularly happy. In my experience, no matter how I may feel about my job on any given day, remembering to be grateful for the fact that I have one immediately both humbles and elevates me. There's always a speck of good to find in any situation, and when you see it, you're looking at the creative force behind us all. Part of my job is customer service, so I have plenty of opportunities to practice this one.

Gratitude for what we have, not resentment for what we don't have, is what makes it possible for us to receive what we want. The act of being grateful raises our energy level and attracts to us whatever is in tune with that higher energy. There's nothing mystical or mysterious about this—it's simple physics.

Radio waves operate in a similar way with their various frequencies. By tuning in to those frequencies, listeners pick up specific signals. In this way, you are like a radio station. If your energy level is at a low frequency, you will pick up the lower-level signals at that frequency, the signals other people are emitting. Do you tend to find yourself in the middle of arguments you don't want to be in and can't figure out how you got there? Are you surrounded by people and circumstances that seem to drag your creative energy down? Changing your habitual thought patterns will change your frequency, and if you change them in a positive direction, with time you won't attract that sort of energy to yourself.

Gratitude to God for the blessings in your life is an instant frequency changer. It's a form of devotion that brings you closer to the source of all good. Start by giving thanks for the positive aspects of whatever circumstances you're in. You'll immediately feel better.

This can be a particular challenge at work, where we're thrown together with people we might not choose to socialize with. You don't have to like everyone. This is an unrealistic goal. At the same time, I don't wish to oversimplify the complex situations we find ourselves in on the job—I've been in them myself. But it's helpful to remember that there's good in every situation. Focus on that good and ride it to a better-feeling place, then practice gratitude to stay there.

Giving thanks for things you don't see in your life but desperately want can be a challenge, especially when you're feeling hard done-by, but this is exactly when it's most useful. Call to mind your vision and give thanks for it. Feel your belief strengthening as a result. If this is new to you, practice it without worrying whether or not you truly believe it. Like an exercised muscle, it will get stronger. Don't give up.

If you feel you simply can't give thanks for the good things in your current or future situation because all you see is your lack of money or time or the necessities of life, stop and look in another direction. Give thanks for the air you breathe, sunshine, raindrops, blades of grass, leaves on trees, the roof over your head. Stop and feel the magnificence of every cell of your body, the way your heart beats, the way your lungs draw breath, the fact that you have the capacity to read these words and understand them, the fact that you're alive at all. Give thanks for paint or music or your dog. Find that thing you can be grateful for and focus on it over and over until you can easily see the other blessings in your life.

What you begin to experience as you practice being grateful is the great abundance within which we live. This abundance is not limited in any way. Where one leaf dies, another grows. It is out of this abundance that you'll be creating your better life, and it is because of this abundance that you don't need to enter into competition with anyone else.

These are a small part of our blessings, and we can be truly grateful for them.

Thoughts and actions for
Give thanks for it.

1. Get into the thank you habit.

Being grateful is a habit you can learn. A very nice, and obvious, way to do this is to say thank you to the people in your life.

Pay attention to the many little things people do for you every day. It's natural to thank people when they hand you things you've dropped, but do you thank them when they're simply doing their jobs, the way you yourself would like to be thanked for doing yours?

If you're out of the gratitude habit, forget how hackneyed this suggestion may sound and just give it a try. Every time you say thank you to someone else, you're saying it to the Great Spirit behind the act and reinforcing in your own heart and mind the value of a grateful response. Just try it and see how you feel.

2. Radiate gratitude.

Once you begin to develop the habit of gratitude, you'll be pleased to see that it takes on a life of its own. Now you can transfer your sense of gratefulness to the more difficult areas of your life.

Cultivate a sense of having been blessed, especially when you're feeling hard done-by. Make it a point to wake up your gratitude during the more boring moments of your day and let it keep you company. A person who is always aware of being blessed is never bored.

Your sense of gratitude will radiate from you like a golden light. People will feel it without knowing what it is, and their lives will benefit. On the one hand, you're cultivating your gratitude in order to consistently attract good stuff into your life, but more importantly, you're doing this because it's a wonderful thing to do.

II. Space and Time

Set the stage for your art

S pace to work, time to work. There's never enough.

I'm here to tell you that it starts in your mind. While you can't change all the physical parameters of your life in one fell swoop, you *can* start changing both your mind and your situation right now, today, and things *will* get better.

Here are some thoughts on these two gnarly problems that never seem to go away.

If we let them, our day jobs will swallow our lives. If you're reading this book, you probably feel your job *IS* your life.

While it's important to keep the creative thread alive while we're at work, and you'll find plenty of ideas for doing that in these pages, we have to keep that thread running when we get home as well. Yet this is where we really feel the crunch, when we stop fulfilling everyone else's wishes and start focusing on ourselves, only to find that we're too tired or busy to do what we want.

Day-jobbers, by definition, are not full-time artists. We most likely have no dedicated workshop, and we certainly don't (yet) have all day to devote to our art. For creative folks who spend most of their waking hours in someone else's employ, the fact of having nowhere to create and no time for it anyway can seem insurmountable.

The way you choose to deal with space and time will set the stage for both your art and your job. Why not apply artistic flair?

Imagine your situation as clay to be molded. Knead it until it's warm and pliable. Keep working it as it changes form. Look at it from as many angles as you can. Approach it with the same problem-solving skills you bring to any other creative project. Ask yourself, "What does this piece need to be just right? Where can I push it or pull it to balance it out? How can I change the tone or better integrate the parts?"

Develop the skill of thinking about your current situation in the same way a writer thinks about a plot or a sculptor thinks about a figure emerging from stone. Objectify it as you would a piece of art in the making. The point is to separate yourself from the emotions that can arise when you perceive your situation as hopeless.

Good art evokes emotion from the viewer, but emotion should not cloud the critical technical skill of the artist. Only by asking at every step of the way, "Does this work?" can an artist produce something that touches the viewer. Use this dissociative skill to assess your situation and make the changes necessary to improve it.

As you read this chapter, remember that, while there is no pill for curing all ills, all change begins in the mind, and the power of your mind is infinitely stronger than the circumstances around you.

Space

When your home is your (WORK)SPACE

Having nowhere to work, no place to call your studio, is a nightmare for any artist. As your mental image of your creative space shrinks, your job expands like a Macy's parade balloon until it fills your life and squeezes you to the size of an ant in the corner.

Resolve right now to honor your spatial needs. Think about what sort of environment would most inspire you and then take the time you need to reorient your home base. What can you do RIGHT NOW to charge your home with creative energy?

Don't wait until you have a full-time studio. If you keep putting it off in your mind, that day will never come. Start now with what you have. You'll feel the effects immediately.

A good friend of mine once shared a story with me that illustrates the close relationship between our inner states and the homes we live in.

One day, my friend woke up with an overwhelming feeling she would soon be moving to another house. She told me she had no reason to move at that time, as she actually liked her little cottage very much. She had no idea where or when she would be going, but she knew it was about to happen as surely as she knew her name.

Compelled to move, she went ahead and packed up all her belongings and waited. For weeks, she lived in her empty cottage, sitting on the floor, leaning on suitcases, walking around towers of boxes. Then suddenly one day she knew, as sure as she had before, that she wasn't going anywhere. So she unpacked her things, got rid of the boxes, and went on with life.

But a lot had changed. When all this was over and she was on the other side, feeling a little silly about the whole thing, she realized that she was in an entirely new place within herself. It was her heart and her mind that had changed, not her home.

For me, this story demonstrates the intricate relationship between our inner and outer realities. Change yourself inside and you'll feel compelled to alter your outside reality; change your outside circumstances—really change them, don't just push a chair to another wall—and you'll experience a change inside yourself as well. Not everyone needs to go to the lengths my friend did, but the principle remains the same.

Here are a few of the ways you can enlarge your artistic territory on a practical level. While some of these things might seem to go without saying, it's possible you haven't seen the necessity for them yet.

What sort of home would support your vision?

Is your living space as supportive of your dreams as it could be? It might be a victim of the bits and pieces we tend to collect over the years, the way comets gather flotsam on their journeys through space. As someone who works with materials of one kind or another, you might be more prone to this than other people.

Set aside a day and rearrange your environment to give your creative work the priority it deserves. A home designed around your passions will immediately begin attracting similar energy, in the same way an artist's studio or craftsman's workshop, or, for that matter, a temple does.

Give more space to the things you love and clear out the things you no longer care about. In fact, clearing out what we no longer need creates the space life requires in order to bring us those new and better things. As a person who tends to move from house to house, I've experienced firsthand the value of sorting through unnecessary stuff on a regular basis.

As you redesign your space, surround yourself with things that give you a kick, whether they inspire you to the heights or challenge your beliefs—whatever it takes to bring you into that creative place.

Take stock and clear away what no longer reflects your interests and ideals. Use your living space as a road map. Remember that your past beliefs got you to your present situation. Clutter reflects who you've been up 'till now. Unexamined clutter can keep you in the past and actually slow down your growth. If you want a better future, surround yourself with things that are reflective of where you want to go.

While you're at it, cut out some of the at-home habits that don't support your creative self. Everyone has their own. Keep a vigilant eye on how you might be sabotaging your own efforts with periods of TV, sleep, and hanging out that eat into your creative time. This includes even the more insidious avoidance habits, such as reading about art instead of making it—an Achilles heel of mine for many years. Everything you like to do has its place in your life; balance is key. Recreate your space with the intention of minimizing the distractions you're in the process of outgrowing.

It may take more than a day to change old habits, but bringing your surroundings into harmony with your goals will do wonders for your attitude.

Could a dedicated workspace change your life?

Setting up a workspace dedicated solely to your creative activity can be hard when your house is crowded or you live with other people, or a cat, but please do it anyway. Squ-e-e-e-ze that space out. You won't be sorry!

A dedicated workspace is one of the most valuable gifts you'll ever give your creative self. Being able to leave your unfinished work lying out so you can stop by for five-minute sessions here and there could mean the difference between a completed project and a UFO.

For most mediums, there's a way to set up a small workspace somewhere in your home, even if it's inside a suitcase that can be opened to access your tools when you're ready. Get creative: a rolling cart, a climbing shelf, a decorative screen to hide a mess. Flexible mats designed for jigsaw puzzles can be adapted. Darkrooms can be set up in the oddest converted corners. How about living room furniture on wheels to easily clear the floor when you're ready to dance?

If your materials are toxic or you're casting bronze, look into a rented shed. You might have to adjust the size of your work for the time being, but there's a lot to be learned creatively from applying undesired limitations to your work.

Once you start leaving your works-in-progress out in the open, with all materials readily available, you'll probably find yourself gravitating to them in a way you can't when they're stuffed in a backpack or a drawer.

You might think that creating a dedicated workspace is possible for everyone but you, and it may be that you're living in a suitcase yourself. Nevertheless, whatever you make room for in your life will flourish. Give yourself a workspace. It will transform your creative process.

What would you pack in a portable studio?

Now that your home is beginning to reflect your creative work, it's probably getting harder to leave it in the morning. Yet the job calls and you must answer.

One solution is to take a smaller version of your workspace with you wherever you go. Some paper and a pen, a small sketchpad, a hand-held tape recorder, a tiny camera—you know best what you need. Smart phones are wonderful tools, sort of like electronic Swiss Army knives.

Packing up isn't the same as staying home all day to write music, but until you've created that life for yourself, being prepared for inspired moments is the next best thing. If you have your tools with you, you're more likely to use them. And anyway, I can almost guarantee that wonderful, unexpected moment under the tree won't happen in your living room.

If your tools are big or intrusive, think about other aspects of your medium that would be more portable, even if you've never tried them before. Carrying an easel to work may not be practical, but a set of watercolor pencils might. If you're an oil painter who's never ventured into watercolor, the challenge of this new medium might be just what you need to jostle you out of your current rut.

I was a weaver for many years, and if there's one thing you can't stuff into your purse, it's a six-harness floor loom. Weavers are notoriously creative at finding smaller versions of their art to carry with them: tiny tapestry looms made of cardboard and straight pins, Japanese braid-weaving looms that sit on your lap, or just yarn to weave with your fingers no matter where you are.

When I knew I'd be relocating from one country to another some years ago but had no idea if I'd have enough space on the other end to set up my equipment, I branched out into beading on bead looms. These were portable enough to use in the living room, yet they were based on the same kind of grid-pattern textile designing used in weaving. Most important to me as a loom weaver, they were made of wood and strings! It was a rewarding decision. I still bead today, long after my floor looms have been set up and dismantled several more times.

Once you've made yourself portable, snatch a few minutes in between: during breaks, on the bus, over lunch. In the beginning, you might find it hard to carve out those creative moments, but be aware that you have your tools with you and FEEL their creative pull. It's the first step toward using them. Intend to use them and you'll find a way to do it. Remember, you're developing a habit that could take some practice.

If you realize one day that you've been hauling a backpack of equipment around with you and never opening it, it's time to reexamine your intent. Don't be afraid to do this. You may find that what you've been carrying around is not the passion you thought it was. I've experienced this as well. It may sound heartbreaking, but finding out where your interests really lie can only be a good thing.

What sort of inspiration could you use?

Inspiration can come from within or without, but either way, it's initiated by us, not strewn by the glitter fairies. Creating an inspiring space is one way to encourage it.

Inspiration from within can come as we go about our day or as we purposely sit in silent receptivity. Creating a meditative corner in your home is one major way to support your deeply creative process. Deep creativity is a much bigger topic than this section is addressing, but please check the reading list in the appendix for titles on this subject. *Deep Writing* by Eric Maisel is one such book, as is *The Spirit of Silence: Making Space for Creativity* by John Lane.

Inspiration from without, however, is something you can easily support as you design your living space. Select things that make you want to strive for the very highest within yourself, images or objects that remind you what you really are: a magnificent spiritual being, a naturally creative soul.

Place messages around you in a language that speaks to your own heart, in places where you can't help but see them. What is it that touches you right where you live and makes you want to be your very, very best? Complement this with things that make you want to buckle down and work.

Things that make you want to work aren't necessarily things you like. They could be reproductions or messages that challenge you, authors who irk you and make you want to argue back (or do better), old works of your own that get under your skin. My painting teacher always said that his wife had an uncanny knack for quietly setting on his worktable exactly that object she knew he'd have to paint before he could go on, like a fresh bell pepper with dew from the garden. Get to know your own triggers—or marry someone who does.

By the way, you can carry some of this stuff along with you on your commute to work as another way to integrate your two worlds. Think of it as packing healthy snacks rather than being caught short and grabbing a candy bar. Feed your mind well and it will perform well for you.

Time

Make peace with TIME

I don't think there's any more distressing issue for day-jobbers than that of time. There's never enough of it. And when we do manage to scrape some together, we're too tired from working to make good use of it.

The major complaint I hear, and experience, is the difficulty in switching gears from day job mentality to artistic creativity when you've only got an hour after dinner and are exhausted to boot. At the moment of frustration, we seem to be juggling creative urge, physical energy, and time all at once. It can be a very dark moment indeed. But please don't give in to the darkness! The time monster can seem implacable, but whatever your situation, there's always a way to improve it.

It's my experience that using the creative principles outlined in this book can exercise the mental and imaginative capacity you need to overcome this difficulty. Like everything else in life, time can be experienced in a new way. Just keep working with the principles and things will change.

In the meantime, here are some things to think about to help jumpstart the time you do have.

What can your creative rhythms tell you?

Start by watching your individual rhythm to see how you can use it to your advantage.

Spend a few days observing your natural creative urges over the full 24-hour cycle. Do you wake up bursting with energy, ready to write a novel just as you head off to work? Or are you the night owl who doesn't get revved up until it's time to clock in for the graveyard shift?

How does your energy ebb and flow throughout the day? When do you feel your most creative or your most reflective? When do you get your second wind? When is your mind working most clearly?

For now, you probably have to spend many of what you consider your best hours at work, and this is unfortunate. But once you have a clear picture of your own natural rhythms, you can tweak your schedule.

After you appraise your patterns, take stock of what you've learned. Is there something small that could be adjusted to ease the pressure? Or does something big need to change? Could you, for example, change to another shift at work to accommodate your needs? Could you drop down to 80%? Just because things have been the way they are for a while doesn't mean they need to continue that way. Sometimes a change is too big or too simple to see. I found that dropping down to 80% in a job I couldn't stand gave me two days in a row for weaving, plus Sunday with my family. It was a doable change that brightened my entire attitude, not to mention my energy level, and made the job easier to like.

If your work schedule can't possibly be tampered with, maybe it's time to consider more fundamental changes. Is your present job really the best one for you? Might you be better off in a job where you can work at night or during the day? Changing jobs might seem inconceivable at first glance, but a new timeframe might be exactly what you need to blossom.

If your schedule truly doesn't suit you and it's impossible to change, then swallow hard and accept it. Keep reading and let's find other ways to solve this dilemma.

Time is flexible. How can you play with it?

Time is like quicksilver, like water, like mud. It changes its character depending on how we perceive it.

Try thinking about time as moldable and shapeable, not rigid and fixed between the numbers on the clock face. Hold it in your hands like a ball of warm clay and squish it around. Move a piece from here to there.

Whatever the parameters of your working day, think about adding time on either end. This may not be as difficult as it sounds.

Certainly, when you're struggling to wake up at 5 a.m., the last thing you want to do is get up at 4:30, but adding a half-hour onto one end of the day and subtracting it from the other is something anybody can do. Once you train your mind and body to accept the new hours, you won't feel it at all.

A subtle shift like this can do wonders for your creativity. Get up a half-hour early, douse your head with water, say good morning to the sun (if it's up), make your tea or coffee, and gently move into your creative work. If being creative at that hour is too much to ask, do something rote that you need to do anyway: scales, sketches, sorting, trawling the town with a camera at daybreak. These few additional moments devoted to your work first thing in the morning can turn your whole day around.

Time can be squeezed out of many corners of the day. If you kept track of everything you did in five-minute increments, you'd probably be shocked at how much time you waste. Become more cognizant of what you might be frittering away. Gather up a bunch of those five-minute blobs and smoosh them together into one big juicy half-hour.

What can you do when your job throws a tantrum?

If your job is like most, it's got cycles and rhythms that wreak havoc on your life. End-of-year financial statements, seasonal deliveries, holiday production schedules. They're intrusive and we hate them, but they can be dealt with. At the time I'm writing this, I'm employed as a full-time reporter for a small-town newspaper. I know whereof I speak.

Once you recognize your job's ebb and flow, work with it. If you know that the last week of the month is always a killer because it's payroll time for the bookkeeper in you, don't expect yourself to be creative during those five days. It's the expectations that'll get you every time. I personally expect nothing—I mean, nothing—from myself on Mondays and Tuesdays. Once the paper's on its way to being laid out (not by me), I'm human again. On Mondays and Tuesdays, however, I issue myself a blanket pardon and play Doodle Jewels. It does me a world of good.

If your demanding time is longer than a day or so and you're so flat you can't think straight, find other, more nourishing ways to stay connected to your creativity. Indulge in what my painting teacher, Jim Rosen, used to call "creative indolence." He was referring to leafing through volumes of masterpiece plates, but you can also engage in some of the less demanding parts of your own process.

Sort through old photographs you've taken or swatches you've woven to get an idea of what to do next. Don't feel compelled to make any decisions when you're that wiped out. Just keep your feet wet. Spend luxurious evenings paging through color reproductions of pottery or paintings, soaking up the vapors. Watch videos of ballet performances and ice dancing. Go see a really great movie. If there's a sport you like, watch a game and get inspired by a display of true endurance and determination. Carried out with intent, creative indolence is an essential part of your life as a creative being.

If you feel you absolutely must generate a product, come up with some related activity that isn't as draining as you would normally undertake. Sit quietly with a lap loom instead of weaving yardage. Write a story that is NOT aimed at national competition. Practice your scales. You could even try out a whole new medium. When was the last time you played with your camera? Finger-painted? Wrote a poem?

Find something to do that keeps you connected, but which also acknowledges that you're a human being, after all.

Being an artist is about producing, but it's also about receiving. Look around and draw inspiration from the world. Take yourself on what Julia Cameron calls "artist dates" with yourself, to thrill and surprise, simply rest, refuel, and charge your battery. It's time well spent.

What if you went straight to your art when you got home?

I hear your wails. How could there be a worse time to try to be creative?

Actually, this pivotal moment—the return from work—is an underestimated opportunity to renew your relationship with your art. You may indeed be too exhausted to create at that very moment, but make the gesture and see.

You can prepare for this by ending your last session at a place where picking it up again will be relatively mindless. If you're writing, for example, make sure your next task is to type in pre-marked corrections, not come up with the next plot twist. If you're a weaver, instead of trying to design, start with something rhythmic and routine, like winding a warp. Grease the gears and slide in gently.

If it doesn't work, go away, do something relaxing and fun, or even necessary, then come back and try again when you've got your second wind.

If it still doesn't work, don't worry. Just keep prodding and nudging this thing until it takes form. For now, just sit with your stuff. Read through finished chapters, leaf through old drawings, hum along with recorded riffs, gently stretch your dancing muscles. Maybe you'll get sucked into something.

Maybe you won't. The important thing is not to heap recriminations on yourself. As long as you're moving forward overall, just accept that some days are like that.

What would deep relaxation bring to your life?

Deep relaxation is not just a feel-good treat for the moment. It's an investment in a better you. It's money in the bank for when you need to think clearly and work well. Get yourself a music CD suitable for relaxation and set aside 20 minutes every day just to sit back and listen.

If you ignore your stress levels, they'll tie you up in such crazy knots that your creative self won't stand a chance. A little bit of time dedicated to washing the tension out of both your muscles and your mind is some of the best time you could possibly spend on yourself.

Relaxing deeply is especially valuable during the day, when your mind and muscles can use a good break. But a nice piece of relaxing music is also wonderful as you're dropping off to sleep, especially if you have trouble letting go of the chaotic events of the day.

Another benefit is that, in those moments of deep relaxation, your mind is very open to suggestion. This is a wonderful time to picture yourself living your dreams on a daily basis.

Want to be a great singer? Professional dancer? Bestseller? If you use your deep relaxation time to feed yourself images of your vision, with or without music, they will become part of your thought system, and each time you put your feet back on the ground, your mind will automatically begin arranging things—such as plans and schedules—so that you can achieve these beautiful goals.

The "take heart" pep talk

Workspace and time are not easy issues, so have patience with yourself as you carve out solutions. Just start right here, right now, wherever you are, and plant those seeds. They can't grow if they never make it into the ground. Deal with things in your present environment while you keep your eye on the goal.

Remember that you're here to enjoy yourself—it's why you took up your creative work in the first place!

Do what you can today. Do the rest when it's time.

III. Survive (and Thrive)

Transform your job into a work of art

Now, let's get down to some on-the-job survival skills. But really, surviving is never enough. If you want, you can *soar* through that job and transform it into a joyful place to be. You can head off to work each day with a light step, knowing that you're able to turn your job into creative fodder for achieving your goals.

Of course, transforming your day job in this way means transforming yourself.

You may not think that you and your day job have much in common. I've had enough of them to know the feeling. Just remember that the biggest factor the two of you share is you. *You* are what you bring to the table. It may seem as if your day job is the Blob that ate Manhattan, but this is worth repeating: the power of your mind is stronger than the circumstances surrounding you.

As the person who works the art and the person who works the job, you have a lot of say in the matter. On the one hand, you could let what you hate about your job infest the rest of your life like a cancer. Or you could do the reverse: grace your workplace with inspiration and style—something you might not see very often on your job—and transform those working hours into an extension of everything you love.

Working in art can teach us valuable skills. It can heighten our powers of awareness and observation, increase our patience, and fine-tune our sense of pure craftsmanship. These skills are transferrable to every area of our lives. If you are growing as an artist, you may well be noticing personal growth in other ways. We're going to take a look at how to apply these skills with purpose and intent so that you can SURVIVE and THRIVE in your workplace.

Make your job into a work of art.

Choose your project

Set the goal

Consider this: no art is created without goals. A goal could be as magnificent as "Finish *Mona Lisa* by Saturday" or as mundane as "Man, I've got to clean my tools."

In art, we are always defining projects. The moment you conceive a project, you set in motion a series of spontaneous goals. The next time you get the urge to make or do something creative, notice how you automatically begin figuring out how to make it happen. You don't have to know *how* to do it. You only have to *want* to do it and your mind immediately begins to make it real. This is your creative nature as a human being.

Directing your creative nature is one skill you learn through making art. Now apply this skill to setting creative goals that put your day job in perspective.

First, let's talk about goals.

Goals are inherently achievable. They are not mirages, and the paths to them are not through endless tunnels. They are also not just for ambitious linear-thought go-getters. Goals are simply practical ways for any of us to get from one point to another. You can set them as small and as close to where you currently are as you want.

If your goals don't make you jump out of bed in the morning singing for joy, you've got the wrong goals. This is because many goals we set have nothing to do with who we really are. Goals set because they're appropriate or logical will end up being boring and impractical. You'll probably forget about them almost immediately, like New Year's resolutions, and over time develop a deep distrust of the process.

Instead, try setting goals that grow naturally from your vision. As you arrive at your vision and foster your belief in it, the first steps will become clear, and you will see what goals to set.

I've followed a circuitous path in this regard. I'm describing it here to illustrate the relationship between our visions and the goals that arise from them. In my experience, I first had to let go of the vision I'd been hanging onto for many years before I could let a new one flourish. Only then could I set meaningful goals for myself.

My own dream has always been much like yours: I want to be creative and enjoy myself without having to go to work for someone else. At the same time, I want to live comfortably in a society based on money. The two parts of this vision had always seemed irreconcilable given that I saw myself as a weaver—not the most prosperous artisans on the landscape.

For years, I struggled, swinging from art to prosperity and back again, never seeing the two in harmony, yet not able to accept one without the other. I set goals that seemed appropriate to my more marketable abilities, such as freelance translation, business writing, and selling articles to magazines, but my heart wasn't in any of it, and I achieved nothing.

Then one day I stopped questioning my dream and said, "Why not? Why can't I want art and money at the same time? Forget the old ideas. Just accept that this is what I want and see what happens."

I don't want to oversimplify this process. It took some time and a lot of letting go to accept my impossible dream. But to my surprise, as I changed my thinking, I found my interests shifting. I realized I wasn't weaving anymore, and over the course of a year, I put my looms away, concentrating on needlework instead to satisfy my love of textiles. Simultaneously, my attention was drawn to an old love of letterpress printing and book arts, both of which perfectly complement writing.

Once I had cleared away the parts of my life that didn't fit anymore, deeper things began to emerge, and I could see how to move forward. I unpacked my tabletop press and started creating a business that included things like linocut, ink drawings, and papermaking, things I had previously seen as too impractical to consider.

This change happened because I was willing to embrace a seemingly illogical vision and allow my image of myself to change. Ideas came flooding in. Big goals began to formulate, and, in a process that was gathering speed, I was able to break these larger goals down into smaller goals, which I am now achieving. At this point, I'm acting on them in a natural way, not because they're goals but because I want to.

Go back to your vision. If it's not inspiring you to set goals, look at it more closely. Is it really what you want? Be open to letting it change. Once you've got it right, I think you'll find that the big goals will become clear.

These big goals may not seem achievable from where you stand right now, so make your more immediate goals things you know you can do. Use the larger goals to stretch, but don't make your immediate goals so impossible you discourage yourself. The first exercise below addresses these smaller, practical goals.

A popular and useful way to think about goals is the SMART system. This system says goals should be:

Specific

Measurable

Achievable

Relevant

Time specific

You can find a lot of information about SMART goals on the Internet. These five qualities make goals easier to grasp and possible to achieve.

Use your goals to get back on the path when you feel yourself drifting through the mindless distractions at work. Show up at the beginning of every shift with the knowledge that you are working on that next goal. It will help keep the day job in perspective. Keep taking your steps and achieving your goals and, eventually, your vision will be more real to you than the annoyances around you.

If you still have qualms about artists setting goals, ask yourself if you believe that artists need absolute freedom from restrictions in order to be creative. This is a myth. Truly productive artists regularly set goals and work toward them with consistency and persistence. Success does not come randomly. It comes with purpose and fortitude, and the most successful artists know this well.

The human spirit yearns for growth and advancement. A day job is only mindless if you allow it to be. A strong, achievable goal will give your everyday activities meaning and clarity.

CHOOSE THE PROJECT

1. There is nothing mysterious to setting goals.

Now that you know where you're going, you need a way to get there. Setting goals can be complex and dumbfounding or very, very simple. Let's take the simple route.

Identify one, just one, next step. It should be something to make you stretch ("Get up in the morning" doesn't count), yet something you know you could achieve if you set your mind to it. Don't be afraid of linear logic, by the way. It's good for you once in a while.

An example of the vision-goal relationship might be your desire to be a famous painter, a vision which is nonspecific but inspiring, while one first goal might be to produce a certain number of paintings for an exhibit on a determined date that motivates you to action.

Some people recommend that you write your goal on a small index card and carry it around to read over and over again throughout the day. I have used this method to help me stay on track and build my belief in the reality of my larger goal. Now I FEEL my goal in every cell of my being.

60

Remember that your goal might take some time to become clear, but once you know what you want, enshrine it in your mind. Your goal should remain untouched no matter what else is going on in your life. You don't need to know how to accomplish it; you only need to decide to do it. I can tell you from personal experience that as soon as you decide on your goal, you will see what to do next.

2. Now comes the fun part—love that goal.

Form an image in your mind of what you want. Picture yourself achieving the goal. Savor the thrill you feel in your gut—that shiver of WOW! up and down your spine that lets you know this goal is right on target. You want to feel this every time you think of your goal. This is your inner compass. It tells you that you love your goal.

If you realize one day that you're dragging your goal around like a dead weight, stop and examine the goal, then make the necessary adjustments. Once you are sure of your vision, never change it. It is true to you. But make sure your goal is keeping you moving forward. Is it too vague? Define it more clearly. Do you find it's not precisely what you want to do? Aim at what you want.

You are here to create the life you love, not the one you think you should be creating.

Practice your discipline

Be persistent

A work of art does not spring fully formed from the imagination. It takes a craftsman's hands to bring it into being. In the same way, your goals need you to act on them in order to be achieved. This may seem too obvious for words. On the contrary, it cannot be repeated enough.

What does it mean to practice your discipline? You just do it. You practice guitar by playing the guitar. You practice painting by painting. You practice writing by writing.

Goals are precisely the same. They are achieved by achieving them. The discipline of achieving goals involves acting on your environment whatever your situation happens to be. If you don't act on your present environment, which environment are you going to act on? Waiting until conditions are "right" before you take action toward your goal makes as much sense as waiting until you're a guitar player before you start practicing guitar.

If you already know how to play the guitar, think about what it took for you to learn. There were probably many times you wanted to throw the guitar against the wall, but you didn't. You kept going, lesson after lesson, until you got it.

Persistence is more important than talent. Many people who are blessed with great degrees of talent never succeed at anything because they give up at the first sign of failure, while many other people who are less talented succeed because they never give up. Persistence can make the difference between life and death.

I don't say that lightly. If you slipped into a crevasse in the mountains, all alone, with no one to pull you out, would you sit there and try to dream your way to the top? At what point would you stop scaling the sides? Would you just curl up and die? How would you know if you'd quit too soon?

You may have a history of giving up on projects and moving on to the next. Crafters, in particular, I think, are like jackdaws, diving at one shiny thing after the next. I can say this with impunity because I am one. Every crafter I know has a closet (or house) full of unfinished projects. But you can train and develop your ability to persist. And it's not that hard.

Napoleon Hill wrote, "Persistence is a state of mind, therefore it can be cultivated. Like all states of minds, persistence is based upon definite causes."

This is such a vital subject that I'd like to look at each of the causes he names in turn and see what we can do to develop them.

Definiteness of Purpose

I started this book off by encouraging you to define your vision because definiteness of purpose is such a cornerstone in our lives. If you know precisely what you want, you're more likely to be persistent in your actions to get it. Knowing what your larger vision is, knowing what your goals are, will give you the motivation to propel yourself forward.

Desire

It's tempting to say that the stronger your desire is for a given thing or position, the more consistently you'll work toward it, but this is not necessarily true. A person can desire something like mad, yet not get himself in gear to make it happen. Remember that, just like talent, desire is not enough. We live in a physical world of physical actions. Use your desire to fuel your persistence in meshing the gears to move you forward. If you stay with it, you will certainly figure it out.

On the other hand, if you're one of those who think they don't desire anything badly enough to work toward it, it's possible this is true, but it's also possible you haven't uncovered that thing you really want. Either way, if you find yourself discontent, which you very well might be if you're reading this book, make sure before you give up. Work with the visioning exercise in the section Picture It. Open your heart and see what's there.

Self-reliance

Remember the section on believing in your vision? Hill has named self-reliance as one of the causes of persistence because, he writes, "Belief in one's ability to carry out a plan encourages one to follow the plan through with persistence." Self-reliance means that you can rely on yourself—in this case, for motivation and follow-through. It is belief in your vision that generates the motivation to continue putting one foot in front of the other until you reach your goal.

Definiteness of Plans

Creating definite plans, even if they're necessarily incomplete, begins to give organization to your formless desires. Think of the value of a road map. You can take off on a trip without a map, with only a general sense of the location of your destination. These trips are fun; I've made them myself. But really, they were trips where it didn't matter much if we got to where we said we were going. It was vacation, and we were having fun. If you intend to reach your destination, however, a road map helps. This doesn't mean you can't change routes along the way, but a knowledge of the roads you have to choose from helps you budget your time as well as money for gas and food. Injecting organization into your journey will help you get there faster and with less stress.

Organization is often a hard point for artistic people, partly because we hold the false belief that it runs counter to creativity, but also because once the ideas start tumbling in, they can rampage and overwhelm us. Let them pour in. Write them down. You don't have to do them all! Stick with it and the real and true ones will become clear with time.

Accurate Knowledge

The more you know about your chosen goal or route, the better. If you keep bumping into walls because you lack knowledge about how something works, you will be more likely to give up. Talk to experts in your chosen field; people love to talk about what they do. You just might find a mentor. Accurate knowledge will also make it easier to organize your thoughts into a feasible plan.

Cooperation

Hill writes, "Sympathy, understanding, and harmonious cooperation with others tend to develop persistence." What does he mean by this? In addition to the benefits we gain by being part of a larger network of humans, I think he is referring to the many skills we bring into play in order to cooperate with one another, such as resilience and flexibility. It is these skills that help us persist along our paths.

This can be a sticky point with artists. We need solitude to work, and we're often of a one-track mind. It can be tempting to hole up with your art, but if you cut the ties between yourself and others completely, you don't benefit from the supportive energy a certain amount of cooperation naturally brings. You don't really want to pull yourself over a mountain by your nails, do you?

As unsocial as you might feel it is your right to be, try to find the balance. Cooperate with others and they will likely cooperate with you. We need each other in order to move forward. Another benefit is that cooperation requires patience, a skill definitely required in order to persist.

Willpower

We use our will to get all sorts of things we want. It's possible you think of yourself as not having any willpower, but maybe you haven't set a goal you truly desired before. Still, even when we desire something with all our hearts, there are those times when we doubt our ability to accomplish the goal. This is where willpower sustains us. Remember the image you've created of your goal and apply your will to staying on course. This is persistence.

Habit

Form the habit of moving forward. Hill says something very interesting in this regard: "Fear, the worst of all enemies, can be effectively cured by forced repetition of acts of courage. Everyone who has seen active service in war knows this." If it's possible through repetitive courage to overcome fear during war, the most nightmarish of all human conditions, then you can overcome any obstacle in your way by repeating the appropriate acts over and over until you've developed a new habit contrary to the obstacle. Talk to anyone who's taken up theater in order to conquer shyness or stuttering.

Persistence is taking one action after the next, like breathing. Simply putting one foot in front of the other can carry you to the end. Think about the very next minuscule step you can take toward your goal. Make a phone call, look something up on the Internet, create a file. It doesn't matter what you do—it will certainly take you to the next thing to do.

Every visual artist knows that the world looks different when you shift the angle of your head. So it is that, as you take one step toward your goal, something else is revealed that you hadn't seen before. Just keep walking.

Thoughts and actions for
Practice your discipline

1. Train yourself to be persistent.

Take the time to look closely at each cause of persistence above and ask yourself if you're doing everything you can to support that cause within yourself. Devise ways to remind yourself to change your behavior. The one factor that made the difference for me between advancing and not advancing was persistence. You do it by doing it. Make sure you do it.

2. Reaffirm your persistence.

Use affirmations to help you develop your ability to persist. Affirmations can train your mind to think in such a way that will cause you to be more persistent. Create a list of affirmations that reinforce your belief in the process and repeat them to yourself, not just when you find yourself in doubt but every day.

Work by design

Act with intention

Intention is one of our most neglected tools, even though we use it every day. We create events left and right without even thinking about it, and they are all born of intention.

Intention is where every action begins. I move my right hand because I intend to move it; it doesn't move me. I have the intention to get out of bed (or not), pour myself a cup of coffee, walk to the car, or take the bus.

With a bit of forethought, we can harness our overlooked power of intention and increase the force of action in our art, in our lives, and especially at our jobs. Holding the intention of our personal goals even while we're at work, when we tend to forget about them, is essential to achieving them.

Maybe you're not the sort of artist who routinely prepares materials or ideas before getting down to work, but I'd like you to imagine those times when you have. If you're a painter, you have to take care of your brushes or they'll dry hard as rocks, so you clean them after every use, or at least make sure they're resting in solvent and ready to be used again. If you're a writer, you might have the habit of stacking your work next to the computer, all ready for the next session. Musicians swab mouthpieces, loosen bow hairs, and replace strings, so that when they're ready to play again, so are their instruments. These are very simple examples, but they illustrate acting with intention.

Your day job demands great preparedness from you: punctuality, appropriate dress, readiness to work. In all this preparation for your job, you may not be preparing yourself in other ways. A day job can be demanding, but you can use your time off to plant seeds of creativity that will affect your working hours.

One very simple thing you can do is to plan tomorrow the night before. Before you go to bed, spend some time imagining the day to come. Intend for it to be a good one. Think about what you can do to make it that way. Picture yourself with a wonderful attitude. See happy surprises lying in wait. Picture yourself open to every opportunity that will bring you closer to what you want. Plant the seeds of a good day tonight.

When we're not aware of our intentions as we act, we have nothing to base our next actions on. Many people go through life this way. If you ask these people why they did a certain thing, they'll say, "I don't know." There's no excuse for not knowing why you do something. In fact, if you're honest about it, looking back, you'll see you DO know why you did it—you may not want to know, but you do. If you apply intention beforehand, you're likely to produce a result you're proud to claim.

Here are a couple of things you can do to make sure you're acting with intention.

Thoughts and actions for
Act with intention

1. Think in threes.

If you have a clear creative goal with a definite end, such as a gallery show or a published book, think about this: What are the three most important things you can do tomorrow to reach this goal? Think about three doable things and write them down. Make sure these three things are NOT "Do the laundry" or "Go shopping." Choose three things that specifically bring you closer to your creative goal.

Make sure you do all three as "first thing" as possible. You want to take purposeful and satisfying steps toward your goal as early as you can so you feel good all day long.

These needn't be big things, by the way. In fact, if you're feeling intimidated, see how small you can make them. If you practice this consistently, I think you'll find they'll grow of their own accord.

2. Day-job with intent.

It's easy to forget your goal when you're at work. This is where you specifically need to stay aware of your goals so that the circumstances of your job don't derail your intentions.

I believe that this action—performing your daily duties while staying focused on your goal—is one of the most powerful actions you can take. There is no way to do this but to do it.

Keep bringing your mind back to your vision and your goal. Do whatever you need to do to remind yourself to bring the image to mind. The more strongly you hold the image of your goal while you do other things, the more clearly you will see opportunities to move toward it.

Use your time well

Create time to create

Time is measured by the hours on the clock, but it's also shaped by the activities you undertake. Like everything else, your experience of time is determined by your attitude.

We all know from our own lives that time can fly like a supersonic jet or crawl like a snail. For my part, I don't think this depends on my activities as much as on my state of mind. I've noticed that time can crawl even when I'm doing things I normally enjoy or fly even when I'm working for someone else. The determining factor is my state of mind in the moment. It's a good thing we have the potential to be in full control of our states of mind.

This control is not that hard to exercise. One alternative is to choose not to be dependent at all on whether time crawls or flies. Determine for yourself that you won't let your circumstances drag you into an endless pit of time. If your job requires your full attention, give it that. But there are often open stretches at a mindless job when you're sweeping, sorting, or stacking that can be filled with reaffirming thoughts of your greater vision.

These stretches of time are perfect for focusing on the positive aspects of what you're creating in your life. If you've taken the time to form a detailed image of what you want, you'll be able to call it to mind whenever you have a moment available at work. Even if you can't squeeze the time out for your art, you can use odd moments to move yourself closer to your goal. Every thought counts.

Ask yourself constantly, "What's the most valuable use of my time right now?" Even if you're sweeping out warehouses, you can still use your time to strengthen your resolve. Don't dwell on how much you hate your job. Take a positive stance instead. Devote your thoughts to your art, your personal development, and your spiritual growth.

Use your commuting time to listen to inspirational tapes or play stress-reducing music. If you're on public transportation, read specialist material on your medium or on art in general. Work on better organizing your plan to move forward. Utilize your time. Don't fall prey to self-pity.

Allowing thoughts of your creative goals to wind through your working day will give the day a shape it wouldn't have if you let your boredom or distaste for the job take over. It's a way of changing the shape of your experience of time. I think of it as creating space for my vision to become real.

That being said, there are a lot of hours in a day. You might be spending most of them at work, and many passages in this book address ways of making the most of both your non-working hours and your breaks. But here's another thought: if you're not already rising at dawn, consider integrating the early morning hours into your schedule as well. Sounds awful, but you might be pleasantly surprised.

Remember, your day job exists within your life, not the other way around. The larger your creative hours are, the smaller your job will seem.

Thoughts and actions for
Create time to create

1. Get up early.

Those early hours can be the most productive time of your day. Just one extra half-hour in the morning can produce a chapter outline or five more inches woven on the loom. The stillness of the early hour makes it a fine time to concentrate.

Please don't discount this idea without giving it a fair try. You can conform to a time schedule of your own making, just as you trained yourself to conform to the requirements of your job. It will take your body a good three weeks to assume a new habit, so give yourself a month of early rising before you pack it in.

Set your morning task the night before so you can get right to it when you get up. Yes, you might have to go to bed earlier the night before. Just keep your eye on the goal and ask yourself what you value more.

2. What to do now that you're up.

I heartily recommend a regular meditation practice. However, if you don't have one and don't want one, use the time to create and reflect.

Thirty minutes is enough for a small gestural watercolor or a flip through the shots you took yesterday. Write in your journal and spend time with your goal. I spend an hour or so every morning before meditation with a cup of coffee, my journal, and whatever reading is inspiring me at the moment. Whatever you do that has your goal as its focus will eventually lead to the achievement of that goal.

This quiet time in the morning is often called the Golden Hour in entrepreneurial circles and most of the big achievers make time for it every day.

Early morning time may be a new habit for you, so be gentle with yourself, but be firm. Be as consistent as you possibly can. This skill will also grow with persistence.

Be constant

Design a ritual

One of the most wonderful gifts a creative discipline has to offer is the constancy of its practice. Steady practice is a beautiful form of persistence.

If you're already familiar with this steadiness from the practice of your own art or craft, you can use your skill to handle the demands of your day job. However, if constant discipline is a new concept for you, the exercise of designing a ritual is something you might want to try.

A ritual serves a couple of interesting purposes. On the one hand, it's a reverent and purposeful act meant to focus your energy and concentration. At the same time, if a ritual is performed regularly, it can act as a metronome, or the steady tick-tock of the second hand through your life—a soft, comforting beat that keeps you on track and moving forward. No matter how crazy life gets, you can count on that special time every day and know you're becoming better for it. A ritual performed once can focus your energy intensely on one thing. A ritual performed regularly stretches through your days like a string of pearls.

There is nothing mystical or occult about a ritual in the way I'm suggesting it. We go through them every day, whether we've designed them or not. My cat and I have fallen into a mundane ritual we perform each evening when she gets her treats. She waits for me to get halfway through the door, then leads me to the cabinet and sits in anticipation. I stick the expected number of treats, one by one, in her mouth and she chomps away. It's fun for me to share this silly thing with her, and it's probably gratifying for her to see how well she has me trained.

I've also noticed that if she gets her treats somewhere else in the house, it doesn't count in her mind because that's not the ritual. Rituals can get to be like that; we just don't feel right unless we do them.

A personal ritual is an intimate and private act, and you can use it to increase your focus on your personal or artistic vision. There are as many possibilities as there are individuals. You might write at a certain time every day or meditate, dance, sing, walk to a special tree, recite a poem, or say a prayer. You might stand quietly before a chosen picture or repeat your affirmations.

At one difficult juncture of my life, I developed a ritual of painting a quick watercolor and writing accompanying words in a small black sketchbook every morning after meditation. It was a promise to myself not to let the creative thread disappear simply because I was struggling with personal issues. When I didn't need the ritual anymore, I simply stopped. I still have that little book, and when I leaf through the pages, I'm reminded of my own tenacity during a hard time. However, a ritual doesn't need to be creative. It only needs to be meaningful to you.

Public rituals offer qualities we can use. In my small town, new businesses engage in the ritual of ribbon-cutting ceremonies, which mark the official beginning of public interaction, like a housewarming party. This idea, the marking of a beginning, can be used privately as well. If you've reached the end of one chapter and the beginning of the next, a privately designed ritual can help you move on by honoring your growth and consecrating your next action. This is a wonderful time to express your gratitude for what you've received.

A regular five-minute ritual in the morning can start your day with an awareness you'll feel for hours. You can make it small and keep it simple. Consecrate that act to your art or your vision or your spiritual growth and do it every morning or every evening before you go to bed. Or you might have something like a special stone you keep in your pocket and fondle in the moments you feel stressed or far from your art to center your mind once again on what's important.

A regular ritual can be a background drumbeat for an otherwise disjointed day.

Thoughts and actions for
Design a ritual

1. Do it today.

Do it with great solemnity or wacky joy, but take it seriously. It's a declaration of your relationship with your art and with your dreams.

It can be as light as a dance to spring or as deep as a prayer. Feel the power of your ritual and let it connect you to what you love. Consider it a promise to yourself. Choose a time to perform it when you're not rushed or having to think about something else. Use this time to remember that you are giving new life to something you love.

2. Remember it.

Take a moment now and then throughout your day at work and remember your ritual. Remember how it felt. This needn't take more than a second. With practice, you'll get better at recreating the intent of your ritual no matter where you are.

This is a simple exercise that accomplishes several things. It will help you strengthen your commitment to your vision. It will give you a reference point for your day. And it will help you remember, even in the darkest moments of the storeroom or archives, who you are and what's really important to you.

Be spontaneous

Drop everything and create

Do not fall prey to the myth that artists must go through life being the victims of capricious inspiration. This is simply not true.

While anyone can be unexpectedly blessed by the muse at one time or another, productive artists cultivate inspiration on a regular basis, often by simply starting to work. You can do this whether or not you have a day job.

One way you can do this is to train yourself through a sort of shock method: stop whatever you're doing and work on your art for ten minutes. I learned this practice from psychologist and creativity coach Eric Maisel when I was training to be a coach myself. You can read more about this exercise in the action section of this chapter.

This is a very liberating skill to have. Imagine being able to leap off the sofa at any moment and set to work! Train yourself to do this and you'll be able to grab those ten minutes from your day job whenever you can, whether you've been filing, taking orders, or loading the back of a truck.

Once again, it comes down to your perception. You've probably gotten used to seeing your day job as a block of time during which you work to the exclusion of everything else. This is why it poses such a threat to your art. The door to the office closes behind you and your creative self is left out in the cold. But it's this kind of thinking that creates the disparity in your life, not the job itself.

Think about it another way: your creativity NEVER stops. You are, by nature, bottled creativity. The hours you spend at work may challenge both your understanding of time and your energy level, but they do not prevent you from being a creative person.

If you've gotten into the habit of creating only when you're home and not when you're at work, this is a positive sign of your ability to discipline yourself. To meet the requirements of your job, you've been turning your creative urges off when they haven't seemed appropriate. Now I'm going to encourage you to expand your self-training by weaving moments of artistic work into your day job in ways that will not get you fired. Learn to turn your inspiration on whenever you want it. This is a skill that will also come in handy on the weekends.

Even during the drudge of a job, everyone gets ten minutes now and then. Ask yourself what you usually do during your break at work. Whatever it is, try instead to carry a pad and pencil or some other portable version of your medium, and as soon as you have legitimate time to yourself, go off and write, draw, compose, design, dream. A lot can happen during a ten-minute break.

Use an analogy from the world of textiles and picture what this practice would do to the fabric of your life. Unfurl a length of cloth in your mind. Imagine that this cloth is a dull mud color. Now weave brightly colored threads into it in any pattern you choose. Each thread is a ten-minute break wisely used. One will not make a pattern, but a thousand can. The more ten-minute breaks you use for working creatively, the brighter the fabric of your life will be.

Thoughts and actions for
Drop everything to create

1.Practice spontaneity.

Set an alarm to go off at a random time. When you hear the alarm, drop whatever you're doing and go create for ten minutes. Do this on the weekends or when you're off work, and don't plead impossibility until you try.

For those times when you're at work, just find the ways that are most compatible with your routine. The more random the timing, the better it will be for your spontaneity skills, but your work comes first. Any ten minutes is better than none at all.

If you'd like to break yourself in gently, start with your coffee breaks and then work on random attacks. Try it once and see how it goes, then try it again and again until you get it. Every time you do this, you're stretching your rusty creative muscles.

2. Remember it.

Teach yourself to take ten minutes when you get home and feel like collapsing. Just at the point you think that all you can do is fall onto the couch, go pirouette for ten minutes or blow your flute.

This will awaken you to the rushing stream of creativity that is always alive within you. It never sleeps; we only think it does. Learn to tap into it at your most challenging moments.

Anyone can do something they love for ten minutes. Prepare your materials the night before. When you get home from work, walk straight to the canvas or tuba and have at it for ten minutes. When you're done, you'll be ten minutes closer to achieving your goal.

Build a studio
Surround yourself with what you love

Creative working environments are very important to artists and craftspeople. We're constantly building studios and setting up workspaces. We do this for a variety of reasons.

To start with, we need to have places where we can work without worrying about dripping paint, blasting music, or not being able to concentrate. It's a time-saver to have our work lying about when it's in progress, ready to be picked up at any moment. And glancing over at our unfinished pieces can help us see how to finish them. These are good and practical reasons.

But there are other, less practical reasons. By and large, we just like having our work hanging around us. We enjoy what we do! It's nice to be surrounded by our work—our colors, our thrown pots, our stacks of printed pages. It's validating for us to see our tools and our products. It feels good to be in our own workspaces, to feel the energy of our own creativity right there in that spot.

All of this is missing at our day jobs. It's not that we can't survive being separated from our studios. We're not hothouse orchids, after all. But a generic workplace atmosphere could be altered a bit to support your individual creativity. The object here, as always, is to break down the barriers between your working hours and the rest of your life by gently weaving that creative thread through even the most inaccessible of places.

While it might not be possible or advisable to adorn your workplace with your art, particularly if you're a musician, there are a number of more subtle things you could do. Think about what you would use your studio for, and imagine what you could do or bring to work that would help bridge the gap. What would it take for you to feel more like an artist at work? How much of that can you reasonably import to your workplace?

Looking back at the practical reasons mentioned above, one of them is certainly valid for your workplace. An unfinished piece, or part of one, could benefit from being placed in an unfamiliar environment. It's possible you might see something you hadn't seen before. The unexpected connections the eye can make might help you resolve a creative dilemma. Those of you who work with sound or movement might have to be a bit more inventive, but give some thought to ways of utilizing your workplace as a support for your process. Can you integrate earphones into your work routine, for example?

As for the less practical reasons, a finished piece can be a great boon for your creative self. Imagine glancing over at something you've made and feeling the thrill of accomplishment in a place where that feeling might be rare.

Thoughts and actions for
Surround yourself with what you love

1. Take your creative self to work.

Ask yourself what would make you feel more of your creative self at work and still allow you to do your day job well.

Everyone in every job has at least two inches of space to call his or her own. It may be a desk or a locker or an entire office. Even if it's a hook for your jacket, do what you can to the extent that you feel comfortable. If you can't decorate a whole office, select a motivational screen saver.

Can you hang some of your work on the walls? The feedback could be good for your creative juices. People are intrigued by art. They want it in their lives. Don't hesitate to share.

2. Solve creative problems on the job.

Think about what you're working on, whatever project you're in the middle of, and see if it's possible to start solving some of your creative problems at work.

Bring a snippet of text to think about between tasks, a piece of clay smeared with two glazes to choose from, a small sketch or a color vignette that wants to grow into a painting. Prop this up on your desk and glance at it from time to time, just as you would do in your own studio.

Many creative problems are worked out on the back burner when we're not paying attention. Glance at it, let it work in your imagination, and ideas will start to churn.

Don't get yourself fired, but explore your limits and see what's fair for all concerned. Just remember that you don't need to be in a studio to do good creative work.

Know what your work is about

Set a theme for the day

What is your work about? What is so important to you that you're designing a whole project around it? What are you exploring?

Are you curious about the dynamics between people? Are you tackling environmental or political issues? Looking at your work in a larger social context can produce pieces that are engaging and substantive.

Even if you prefer to explore your medium in a more follow-your-nose way, you still might be addressing questions concerning the qualities of your medium or the role your audience's perception plays. Are you interested in the nature of color or the relationship between sound and clay or wood? How have masters of the past or present addressed these issues? Working within a greater artistic dialogue is essential for us as maturing artists.

Anyone working in any medium, no matter how skilled or unskilled, is working with expression and can benefit from this exercise. Ask yourself what you want to convey in your art. What is it you want people to feel when they see or hear it? What mood can you evoke to communicate this theme? What colors, what words, what notes, what movements?

You probably already ask yourself these things while you're working creatively. Now take the questions to work with you. Create a mental backdrop for this environment that you may not think of as supporting your art. The answers form the building blocks of creative work, and there's no reason you can't continue to build while you're on the job.

Picture this: You're walking along a beach, concentrating on picking up stones. Despite the mosaic of seaweed, shells, and bits of polished glass on the sand, stones are the only things you see as you move from one to the next, intent on your task.

This is the powerful filter of your mind at work. Use it as it was meant to be used. Notice the bits of flotsam that wash up on your shore, but instead of collecting everything, select only those pieces that benefit you and your art.

I've noticed that as I make the change from an intense interest in textiles to a focus on letterpress and printmaking, I'm seeing different things at work. The office hasn't changed, but I have. I still see fabric, of course, and the same aesthetics catch my eye because this is who I am. But they have a different flavor, and I find myself collecting the shiny things around me with a different intent.

A work of art cannot be about everything. Those that try to embrace it all dissolve into chaos and cease to communicate. Ask yourself what your work is about. Notice where the themes in your art are the same as the themes in your life and where they diverge. Highlight what you want to express and let the rest go.

Begin the day by concentrating on what's important to you. The more you can work with heightened awareness and sensitivity to your process, the more enjoyable your time on the job will be. Here are a couple of ways to engage your artistic filter while you're at work.

Thoughts and actions for

Setting a theme for the day

1. Collect pieces of your environment.

Think about the parts of your favorite works of art that really excite you. Set one as a theme for the day. Maybe it's the way a certain painter catches the perfect light or the way a certain poet surprises you with his words. Hold the image of that light or those words as you would hold the image of stones on the beach, and notice anything that resonates.

As you go about your day, look for snippets of dialogue, facial expressions, falling shadows, whatever evokes the themes that interest you. Examine them at home at the end of the day. They're grist for the mill.

Or you could set yourself the challenge of concentrating on one quality (happiness, courage, wistfulness) and being aware of it each time it appears in interactions throughout the day. Be aware of what it called up for you. What was the word spoken, the gesture made? What were the elements that you could use in your own work to evoke a similar quality?

2. Address specific issues in your current work.

Focus on a question you have about your current work and use the surroundings at your day job to answer it. For example, decide that by the time you get off work, you'll resolve the dilemma of Chapter Three, bridge the gap between the first and second acts, come up with a better rhyme for your refrain, or figure out what's wrong with that color in the left-hand corner of that landscape you're painting.

Formulate the problem in the morning and let the filter of your mind sift through the daily data over the course of the day, extracting what's helpful. Glean clues from the job world to bring back to the studio. Wherever you are, your environment is a goldmine of information.

Work deeply

Practice relevance

How often do you wake up in the morning and wonder what the world of insurance (or plumbing or noodle-making) has to do with you?

As human beings, we each have a sense of who we think we are and a more or less well-defined self-image. If the things we do in our lives correspond to who we think we are, the more relevance we see in them and the more they reinforce what we understand ourselves to be. This makes us feel good. A day job as a reporter, for example, makes sense in my life because of my comfort with the writing process and my love of paper and ink.

But the reverse is also true. We all know how uncomfortable it can be to venture into completely unknown territory. We feel like fish out of water when a given activity is too far from how we see ourselves. This perception can make it very difficult to find relevance in our day jobs.

We've all experienced these uncomfortable day jobs. For five years, I worked in a huge corporation, the second-largest reinsurance company in the world. Personally, I was so divorced from the world of insurance that it took me a good year before I understood what my job was about. I cried every night for four years, and I only made peace with the job a few months before it was time to leave it. I say this to show that I do understand.

As artists and craftspeople, we strive to make meaning of the experiences in our lives and to express that meaning to other people. We automatically search for relevance, and when we don't find it, as in our day jobs, we can experience boredom and discontent.

This is where I would encourage you to approach your day job as an art project. Searching for relevance there can take you deeper than you may think your job goes. Working deeply is about finding what's beneath the surface. Uncovering hidden gold is particularly rewarding when there's no reason to think there's anything there at all, like finding oil beneath a barren desert floor.

Think about the relevance your day job might hold for you and what it might have to offer your life. If you have a sense of creative irony, you just might enjoy this assignment. Anyone can describe the similarities in things that are alike or the differences in things that aren't. A much more intriguing exercise is to find the similarities, or relevance, in things that are very different.

Take this exercise seriously enough to do it conscientiously. It can lead you to your deepest values, your core beliefs and, if you do it honestly, you will learn even more about the truth of your art.

My day job at a small-town newspaper is about a lot of things, including human drama and questions of journalistic ethics. It's caused me to think deeply about certain issues in a way I hadn't before, such as the history of our country and the direction it's headed. It's given me the opportunity to ask myself what my beliefs and values are in this regard and how this knowledge can benefit my art.

For one thing, it caused me to see a novel I'd been working on in a whole new way. It deepened the storyline and showed me that I actually wanted to write for an adult audience and not for tweens. Most fun of all for me was that I recognized the true context of the story, and I was able to place it historically. It suddenly made much more sense.

To the creative mind, a working environment can be just another place to gather information and discover self. Search for the things that interest you and connect to your artistic work. Practice seeing your values reflected everywhere. Remember that your past decisions have brought you to the place you are right now. Your day job is just one of many circumstances you've created for yourself. You may not feel like claiming this job, but you will find your beliefs reflected in it.

Until you can change it, let it support your art, and have fun with it.

Thoughts and actions for
Practice relevance

1. First, objectify your job.

This will allow you to see your day job as a project in its own right and help you separate yourself from it. Think about the job as if it were a painting on the wall. What are its characteristics? Is it about environmental conservation, death and dying, putting order into chaos (commonly known as filing)?

The point is to see the context of your job within the larger context of society, not simply as an extension of yourself.

2. Now connect the dots.

Think about your vision or the goal you've defined. In your mind's eye, place your vision or goal next to your objectified day job. Place them at arm's length, where you can get a good look at them. Describe the similarities. Write them down.

Pretend that these two things, your vision and the job, are two paintings you're looking at. Ask yourself questions like, "What is the theme of each? How do they relate to one another? What are the dynamics between the two?"

Look for the connections, not the differences. The differences are easy. Once you begin to see the connective factors, the job will appear much more valuable to you.

Work lightly

Be joyous

It's a challenge to create joy where you think it doesn't exist, like it's a challenge to be inspired when you're not. But just as you can manufacture inspiration, you can manufacture joy. In fact, to get to inspiration, you've got to lighten things up.

Contrary to popular belief, inspiration does not come from the depths of depression or the bottom of a bottle. Creative inspiration comes in those moments when we pierce the darkness and allow the light to shine through thick clouds. Nothing promotes the piercing of darkness more than joy, and joy, like everything else, is a result of the way we think.

If you want to experience inspiration in your art and joy despite your job, you must change the way you think. Every chapter in this book is dependent upon the message in this one.

James Allen was a British writer who lived between the years 1864 and 1912, when the philosophy behind the power of thought was being explored. In 1902, he published a small volume called *As a Man Thinketh*. In it, Allen writes:

"Man is made or unmade by himself. . . . By the right application of thought, man ascends to the Divine Perfection; by the abuse and wrong application of thought, he descends below the level of the beast. Between these two extremes are all the grades of character, and man is their maker and master."

He goes on to say, "Every man is where he is by the law of his being; the thoughts which he has built into his character have brought him there. . . . Man is buffeted by circumstances so long as he believes himself to be the creature of outside conditions, but when he realizes that he is a creative power, and that he may command the hidden soil and seeds of his being out of which circumstances grow, he then becomes the rightful master of himself."

Pretty heavy stuff for a chapter on lightness of being, but I hope the point is well taken.

You alone create the lightness or darkness in which you live. If you apply positive thinking to your daily routine, your entire feeling about your job will change and, over time, so will the circumstances.

I can't stress enough the power of your mind to create joy. If you see your job as drudgery, only you can change this experience. It's no use saying, "But there's no way out." Say instead, "I intend to create joy in my life. Now how can I do that?" Open your mind to the possibilities. Use your creative skills to find a solution. There is always a way. You should know this from your art.

Let's think about it like this. Everything around you, and including you, is a manifestation of energy at a particular level of vibration. This is no longer disputed by science. As an artist, your medium may appear to be paint or words or movement or sound, but as a creative being, your medium is energy. Stop for a moment and feel your ability to affect your energy field. Just for a moment, feel the sad, depressing energy you may be used to (but don't get stuck there). Now turn the knob and think of something positive, something you love, something that makes you happy. Feel the difference. It's that simple.

Inspiration and joy are states of mind, and states of mind are vibrations. Learn to shift into a positive vibration at work. Use your thoughts to bring in the light. Everyone has this ability. If you find yourself still stuck in the darkness, ask yourself how you're benefiting from the situation as it is, then decide if that's something you truly don't want to change.

"All that man achieves," Allen writes, "and all that he fails to achieve is the direct result of his own thoughts. . . . A man's weakness and strength, purity and impurity, are his own, and not another man's; they are brought about by himself, and not by another; and they can only be altered by himself, never by another. His condition is also his own, and not another man's.

His sufferings and his happiness are evolved from within. As he thinks, so he is; as he continues to think, so he remains."

Resolve to not remain in a condition you're not satisfied with. As conditions go, I recommend joy.

And bring it to the workplace. This is one of the ultimate challenges for a day-jobber. If you can create joy in your day job, you can create it anywhere. And if creating joy teaches you to create inspiration, your whole life is blessed.

Thoughts and actions for
Be joyous

1. Create joy.

Try having some fun. Fun can really jog the energy and get it moving in a more creative direction. Listen to music, if you can. If you work at home, pet your dog. Open a window and breathe in some fresh air. Walk around the hallways and pirouette when no one's looking. Tell a joke and make someone smile. Pack yourself an unusual lunch. Have cappuccino instead of tea.

Fun is everywhere in this delightful universe. Plan a reward for when you get home: a hot bath, a good meal, a rollicking comedy. Laugh! Relaxing into laughter or contentment renews the connection with your creative self, and it can be as refreshing as a nap. Clear the fuzz and blast through the cement ceiling in your head.

Welcome in the sunshine and let the energy flow. Invite it in and learn to dance!

2. Explore the joy of inspiration.

Use your imagination on this one, and get silly. Picture piles of fairy dust lying around and wave your hands through them as you walk by. Stash a pile by the filing cabinets, the storage closet, the archive basement. These are your secret stashes of fairy dust. Watch it ripple as you pass by.

Know that your inspiration is lying around like this, too, in secret corners, along the hall, in the cash register. You never know where you'll find it. Smile when you find a pile. Practice stirring and smiling until you laugh out loud. Inspiration is that easy. Let it take you back to when there was no day job, no dark clouds, just crayons and fairies. This is still you.

Learn to think of inspiration as a joyful thing, accessible and available, piled up everywhere, especially at work!

Learn your craft

Cultivate patience

One of the marks of a great craftsman is the ability to allow a work to emerge in all its fullness and maturity. Because this ability requires quiet patience, I see the craftsman inside me as a refuge from a world gone mad. Are things moving too fast for you? Stop and talk to a craftsman.

The craftsman clearly recognizes the time each piece needs in order to evolve. The craftsman knows that, if he lets it, what he's working on will morph over time into something that is deeper and richer than the original idea. The craftsman understands how essential it is to take the time to rub and sand and polish all the rough edges of his raw material into a fine and valuable object.

Time is a major function of art. We miss so much when we rush through projects, like the surprising insights we could gain into the meaning of the work or the natural movement into deeper levels of understanding. If we go too fast, we miss learning the true significance of the process we thought we were controlling. All this can be seen if we only wait and watch and listen. This takes great patience.

Master artists whose works have endured to touch the hearts of people throughout the ages were great craftsmen as well. The endurance of their art testifies to this. Hastily produced work whose depths have not been explored will not stand the test of time, either in ideas or materials. Great artists are patient artists.

And great gardeners are patient gardeners. They know that there's a gestation time for every seed, a time during which breathtaking changes are occurring beneath the soil. They know that just because you can't see it doesn't mean it isn't happening. Every seed has a built-in germination time that cannot be rushed except at our peril.

And so it is with your goals. You plant a seed with the setting of a goal, and you nourish it with every supportive thing you do thereafter. Every thought and exercise in this book is aimed at helping you cultivate your seed into a plant you can harvest. Of course, as all farmers know and many teachers point out, sowing and reaping occur in two different seasons. Just as with a tree, if you plant an idea today, you must wait for it to mature before you reap its fruit.

How long will it take you to reach your goal? No one knows. It could be sooner or later than you imagined. Your goal is a growing thing. It's tempting to try to nudge or even force a growing thing to completion, but if we push and pull and twist, we can end up destroying something that would have matured in its own time with far less worry and far greater benefit.

I'm talking about art and life goals, of course, but I am also talking about you yourself. You are a work of art. Have patience with yourself as you grow. You may want nothing more than to quit that job today. But before you leave yourself in the lurch, make sure the time is right. Be wary of rushing to reap what has only just been sown. Keep your mind on your goal. Do everything you can to nurture it along. Work with it, water it, study it, and know that it will bear fruit.

Thoughts and actions for
Cultivate patience

1. Learn by doing.

If you make a decision to cultivate patience, chances are excellent that you'll be hit with an avalanche of annoying events that will try your soul. On this planet of ours, we learn by doing, and if all you see is your own impatience the moment you ask to be patient, you're probably on the right track.

I don't think any aspect of life gives us as much on-the-job training as patience. Learn to take advantage of every opportunity that comes your way. It's not called "exercising patience" for nothing.

As you're working for your larger goal, you will still be in what look like smaller circumstances. When you're facing a trying juncture, stop and breath. Count to ten and remember that you're in training. You're adding a building block to your artistic skill set. Accept the challenge as a gift and feel yourself become bigger and better in that moment.

2. Trust.

Perhaps the most important lesson we can learn in life is to trust. Impatience is very often a symptom of not trusting: We need to see the outcome; we need to know it's going to be okay.

Well, it *is* going to be okay. Practice believing this. Everything is moving toward the greater good, whether it looks that way to us at the time or not, and it's up to us to move with it.

A good way to cultivate patience is to stop and give thanks for the bumps—and we've made a full circle to gratitude. Your act of giving thanks for the lessons you're learning will begin to dissipate the irritated energy of impatience.

Remember that, as a craftsman, you trust the creative process. Apply the same trust to the process of your life and let your job benefit from this wisdom as well. Everything in our world changes, without exception. Exercise your God-given patience to learn when to act and when to wait. Be still. Watch. Trust.

IV: Escape

Create a masterpiece of yourself

This section is about how to grow out of your present position and into a better one by intentionally creating a better, larger You. We're shifting the focus from "out there," (i.e., your home space, your workspace, your job, and your art), to "in here," where the change has to take place.

I think of it as creating masterpieces of ourselves because I think of us as the works of art. Intentionally working on ourselves calls for the fullest powers of our creativity. It asks us to be disciplined, to harness our wills, and to apply our fortitude to overcoming difficult challenges.

Shifting the focus from changing our outer worlds to changing our inner worlds parallels the movement from the level of artisan's apprentice to the level of master craftsman, where the craftsman is now in control of every aspect of his work. Just as an artist outgrows early experiments and goes on to produce works of true art, it's possible for a day-jobber to shrug off the current job, or the necessity to have one, and walk confidently into a greater reality that realizes greater potential.

My own experience with early day jobs was dismal. The positions I found myself in didn't correspond to any idea I had of myself, and some of them were truly awful. The oil refinery comes to mind. And no matter what dreadful job I found myself in, I was convinced I'd be there forever. One could say it was hell. And it wasn't until I intentionally began to change inside that my outer circumstance began to change.

If you're even remotely interested in the subject of this book, you're much farther along than I ever was. Whatever you do, don't give up. If you stick with it, your present circumstance will surely change into something that more closely resembles your desires for yourself. It's a dance between your desires, or your artistic vision, and the reality of your world, or your raw materials. Draw on your greatest skill and very best artistry. Stay with it and believe in yourself. Be persistent. You can do this.

Overfill your present life

It's a great temptation to slack off in a job you don't like. Motivation is low, and you're probably in a field you don't want to advance in anyway.

But let's pretend for a moment that you do like your field. We all know that if you want to be promoted in a field you like, you have to do more than just a good job. If you do a good job, your boss is likely to keep you where you are. You have to do a job that's qualitatively bigger and better than your present position. You have to "overfill" your position so that your potential will be recognized.

But what if you're in a field you don't want to be in? Even if you feel like a round peg in a square hole, the principle remains the same. To move to a circumstance you want to be in, even if it's in a completely different field, like moving from being an oil refinery lackey to being an author, you still have to overfill your present positions, both in the oil refinery and in writing.

A good place to start is by remembering to keep your day job in perspective. Your day job occupies a small percentage of your universe. Life is bigger than your job, and life loves increase and expansion. The laws of nature respond favorably to the intention of advancement. They do not respond favorably to the dillydallying of a slacker.

Think about all your unfulfilled plans and dreams. Feel them hovering about you like phantom limbs, ghostlike extensions of yourself that have no life force to sustain them. If they're limp and slack like deflated balloons, it's because you don't believe in them.

Now imagine a larger you, one whose plans and dreams are as concrete and clear as your day job is right now. Picture pumping life force into those limbs like blood through veins. Imagine moving through life as this larger, more vital person whose plans and dreams are real and alive.

To go back to our analogy of moving from apprentice to master, becoming a master craftsman is not just a matter of *doing* more; it's a matter of *being* more. Master painters and composers create works of greatness because they know their art and craft in all their cells. It's knowledge beyond idea; it's knowledge of being and doing. As an aspiring master of your life, use your imagination on yourself. See yourself the way you want to be. Claim your plans and dreams as your own.

Do the greatest, most complete job at work that you can, not because you necessarily want to be promoted, but because you want to be great. Overfill your present position at work and you will be auditioning, so to speak, for a better part in life and art, a part that requires higher-level skills.

Overfilling your present life is about making qualitative changes in awareness and action. In the process, you'll be developing your imagination, your intuition, your perception, your memory, your reason, and your will. These are the faculties that separate us from the animals. Their development is what separates the dillydallying slacker from the advancing human being.

Thoughts and actions for
Overfill your present life

1. Become aware of your presence.

Sit quietly and feel your own energy. What is its quality? Is it whirring like a bumblebee, flowing like a soft brook, blinking like a swarm of lightning bugs? Is it thick and warm like honey, calm like a cool breeze, or edgy like a honking horn? What does it feel like?

Don't worry if you've had ten cups of coffee or just run a marathon. This is the energy that is you at this moment, right now. Learn to stop periodically during your day and feel your energy. Check up on it and see what it's doing. See if it's serving you or not. If it's not—if it's too edgy or too scattered—change it. Or next time don't drink that coffee.

At the same time, use your invisible feelers to get a more accurate reading of your larger self. You're much bigger than you look. Try to locate the borders of your self. Now imagine expanding your energy into the farthest reaches of space, all the way out as far as you can feel. This is not even one-gazillionth of how big you really are.

2. Overfill your job.

Throughout this book, I've been encouraging you to apply your artistry to your day job. Now tighten up and elevate the use of your skills. Notice when you have the tendency to let things go at work because "it's just a job." This is the slacker talking, and if you act like a slacker, the universe will treat you like one.

In his little book, *The Science of Getting Rich,* Wallace Wattles, who was focusing specifically on creating wealth and success, said this:

"Do all the work you can do, every day, and do each piece of work in a perfectly successful manner. Put the power of success and the purpose of getting rich into everything that you do. . . . Do not try to more than fill your present place with a view to pleasing your employer. Do it with the idea of advancing yourself."

No matter what your job, acting with the consistent intention of overfilling it will make you a greater person. The universe will respond to this and you will advance, if not in this job, then in another, where you are a better fit. Move through your days with the intention to outgrow your present job, not because you hate it, but because you are becoming a greater person.

114

Do the day completely

Here's a practical way to begin overfilling your present position. Doing the day completely means doing everything that can possibly be done today. A day in which not everything has been done is an unfilled day. In order to move on in life, you want to fill every day with as much quality, not quantity, as you can.

A day can be thought of as the numbers on the clock face, or it can be experienced as the continuing flow of the actions one takes. If you opt for the former, the day can drag like a ball and chain. If you opt for the latter, your perception of time will alter vastly according to the quality of your actions.

Think, for example, about something you've recently done in a haphazard, sloppy, offhand way. This was probably because you had no real desire to do it. Now think of something you've done that you sincerely cared about and enjoyed doing. The face of the clock might show you a similar number of minutes allotted to each activity, but your experience of the timing will have been very different.

As you recall these two activities, you probably notice a difference in your gratification level. A day of sloppy, offhand actions will result in a sloppy, offhand day. If your days are lining up like this, you might feel you're standing still, but in fact, you're sliding backward. There is no standing still in nature. If you're not moving forward, you're moving backward. Enough of these days in a row will put you off the map.

Leave no work undone. This does not mean to run yourself ragged with stress, staying up to all hours and packing in the work until you break down. But it does mean to work conscientiously and efficiently, completing every action with care and grace, doing all that needs to be done and nothing less.

Sometimes, it also means doing nothing more. I went through a terrible time many years ago with a difficult physical condition called fibromyalgia. Among other things, it left me exhausted, in pain, and often incapable of completing the simplest tasks. During this time, I discovered that it was better for me to make a list of the things I had done that day than to start the day with a list of things I should do but probably couldn't. Every morning, I started with a blank sheet of paper, and each time I got something done, I put it on the list. Some days, there was only one thing on the list, but I knew I had done it to the best of my ability. That time is behind me, but the lesson I learned was valuable. The name of the game is quality, not quantity.

There's a lot going on behind the scenes of your actions that you can't see. You've got your vision, you've set your goal, and you're taking steps in the right direction. You're doing what you can do from where you are, and life is moving to meet you. However, if you don't do all that you can do, if you falter on your side out of laziness or negligence, it's likely that things will falter correspondingly on the other side. Certain people might not come your way, essential elements might not move into place, and important connections might not be made.

Do your part by filling your day with everything you can do, as efficiently and completely as you can. This includes saying things you might feel need to be said. If you've been meaning to talk to someone, about anything at all, make sure you do. If you're on the phone and feel moved to say thank you for something the other person did or to set a lunch date you've been meaning to set, do it. You never know what will come out of the smallest actions you take.

At the very least, this is one day you won't be regretting at the end of your life. And you'll have the satisfaction of knowing that each and every day completed in this way contributed to making you the success you became.

Thoughts and actions for
Do the day completely

1. Take a deep breath and slow down.

Rushing through life is no way to create quality. We are all guilty of shifting into automatic at one time or another and zooming to the end of the task, leaving unfinished details flying in the wind. One step toward doing the day completely is consciously slowing down and injecting quality.

Every time you notice that your feet have left planet earth, stop and take a deep breath. It's almost too obvious for words, but how often do you do it? This simple action can bring you back to the center, where you belong.

Breathe in, and as you breathe out, feel yourself centering. Feel your shoulders relax and your head clear. Remind yourself of the quality you're aiming at. Think about what you're doing. Set your priorities. Start again calmer and more focused, and better able to do the job.

2. Pare down your obligations.

"My day is already overfilled!" you cry. You feel as if you can't stuff one more thing into those 24 hours. And you're right. You shouldn't. The point is not to overfill with actions but to overfill with quality. It's better to do fewer actions of exceedingly high quality than a multitude of poorly executed chores.

Reevaluate your obligations and start paring down where necessary. Keep only those that serve you well. Once you begin eliminating items from your to-do list, you'll be amazed at how many of them were not necessary at all. Examine closely everything you've committed yourself to, and if it's tearing you down rather than building you up, ask yourself how truly necessary it is. Think about how many "essentials" don't get done when you're home sick—and doesn't the world keep going round?

Hold your vision

If you aren't crystal clear about what you want for yourself, it won't be possible to achieve results. It's worth repeating that you must turn your clear vision into a concise statement that your imagination can take hold of. Your vision is a stepladder out of your day job. Without a vision, it will be hard to go anywhere, which is why this book started precisely at that point. Now we're revisiting the idea of a vision for the purpose of overfilling your job.

Visions are beautiful and useful at the same time. Remembering your vision will inform your decisions and keep you on track. One entrepreneur compared it to looking up at the top of the mountain as he climbed the path. While there's no getting away from the underbrush, a periodic glance at the mountaintop raises your spirits and reminds you where you're going.

But your vision is more than a guide over rocky terrain. It's a VERY BIG IDEA that you can use to fill your present situation and move yourself forward through your actions to your goal.

All craftsmen begin with a vision of some sort, but master craftsmen never let it go.

Use your vision as the tool it's meant to be. Hold it in your mind as you sweep the floor or stock the shelves. Instead of worrying about leaving your job, let your vision permeate your present reality as if it were ink on blotting paper. Let it seep into every pore of your being. Imbue it with the energy of your belief in it. This energy will charge your present circumstances and start the process of drawing toward you everything you need for your vision to be fulfilled.

If you use your vision in this way, your life will automatically begin to reflect your intention. This might be visible in small ways at first, but they will grow into increasingly big and surprising ways as you attract your new life to yourself.

Practice holding your vision for your life in the same way you hold a vision for a piece of art or a new project, but now, as a master craftsman, hold it more strongly, more completely, and more confidently than ever before. Hold it in your mind's eye and in your heart. Hold it in your whole body, in every cell, in your whole presence. Live within it and let it inform everything you do.

As you become more skilled at holding your vision and living through it, like a master craftsman, you can adjust and tweak and coax it into being.

The bigger and more saturated your vision becomes, the smaller your job is going to seem. There will come a point when your job will slip off by the wayside. You might not even notice it's gone.

Thoughts and actions for
Hold your vision

1. Visualize, visualize, visualize.

Visualization is essential to holding your vision. Deepen and strengthen your skills. If you're used to letting good and important ideas fly through your mind, it's time to learn to hold them steady. Treat your imagination as one of your tools and really work with it. Imprint your cells with your vision and they will hold it for you.

Generate the juicy details. If you dream of being a professional photographer, visualize your darkroom or digital system, see yourself on assignment and published in a travel magazine. Smell the chemicals, hear the whirr of the mechanism. If you want to be on stage, feel the warmth of the lights and hear the rustle of the audience behind them, the applause at the end of the first act. See yourself performing "that play."

Spend some time every day devoted to this exercise. Just close your eyes and dream. Now make sure your goals grow directly from that juicy vision. Soak yourself in the details. This is so vital that it can't be stressed enough.

By the way, this works with money, too.

2. Imbue your presence.

Pause and get a sense of your own presence and energy. Really feel it.

Now think of your vision and notice any changes in how you feel. Did your sense of your presence get bigger or smaller? Did it change in quality? Be aware of your presence, enhanced by your vision, throughout the day. "Be" a published novelist as you deliver mail or wipe the counters. Do this until it becomes second nature. You're imbuing your presence with a new quality and generating the energy that will attract your future to you.

For a while, you'll be doing many of the same things at work that you've been doing, but you're learning to do them in a different way. Soon, the things you do will be different as well.

You're that much closer to overfilling your present position.

Move with purpose

Acting on your vision and your goals will move you forward, but if you want to propel yourself into another orbit, ignite your actions with a sense of purpose.

A sense of purpose is the result of having a clear and desired goal. But simply having a goal doesn't make you act with purpose. If this were true, everyone would be jumping into orbit all the time. Most people, I think, spontaneously act with purpose at different moments in their lives, but holding to a focused sense of purpose for a specific goal over a long period of time is a skill one has to work at developing.

It's worth the effort. Acting in this way will help bring your vision into reality, but it will also help you create yourself as both the master craftsman and the masterpiece.

Watch a master craftsman at work. There's not one unnecessary movement. His mind is completely focused on the end result. He's moving with purpose.

The craftsman may no longer be aware of this. His movements are so familiar to him, his confidence so complete, that he is in total control. His ability to move with purpose is so deeply ingrained in his being that it's become part of him. It takes tremendous dedication and intent to reach this level, but the moment he started training himself in his purposeful action, the craftsman's work began to take on a deeper quality.

You probably know what it feels like to be purposeful in conceiving a project but unable to sustain it afterward. How often have you bounced off the walls with enthusiasm as you described a brilliant idea to anyone who listened and then gone on to move almost absently through your daily routine, and possibly also when it came time to act on the project? It might be a new feeling for you to have a sustained sense of purpose. Learn to recognize it, to generate it at will, and to imbue all your actions with it.

Practice this combination of action and purpose no matter what you do. Let it power your life. This is not to say that you should explode with unrelated enthusiasm every time you answer the phone at work. You'll scare away the customers. It's just to say that your quiet purpose, your unruffled belief in yourself, will make every action a step towards your goal.

Moving or acting with a sense of purpose represents a qualitative change in daily activities that still seem normal and familiar on the surface. However, these actions are now enriched. They'll look very familiar from the outside, but they'll be very different in quality. And while you yourself might not feel different a first, the effects of purposeful action will pile up like autumn leaves. Don't let yourself be discouraged by a seeming lack of results. It takes time to change circumstances that have been manifesting over a period of years.

Thoughts and actions for
Move with purpose

1. Write a mission statement.

Companies write mission statements to help them define key aspects of their operations, from the kind of business they're in to their goals and objectives. Craftsmen probably don't write mission statements unless they're also businessmen, but this doesn't make mission statements irrelevant for artists. Writing a custom-made mission statement can help you get a better handle on your purpose so you can throw it behind the things you do.

Ask yourself why you do your art and what you hope to get out of it. Are you aiming at selling your work? Who are your customers? What sort of image do you want to convey as an artist? What do you want to produce? What's the philosophy behind your work? What drives you as an artist and a human being?

Questions like this can help shape your idea of your purpose and remind you why you're contending with a day job in the first place.

2. Recognize your sense of purpose.

As I write this section of the book, it's baseball season. I don't think you could ask for clearer examples of people acting with specific purpose than athletes. A batter doesn't just want to hit the ball; he wants to hit it in a certain way to fulfill his purpose at the plate. He's batting in a certain order on his team and under certain circumstances created by the game. He needs to bunt to a certain place in the field or to send that ball sailing right between the outfielders.

Likewise, as an author, I don't want to simply write a book; I want to write a book that's truthful, helpful, and clear at the same time. I have a complex purpose that I've boiled down to a recognizable feeling, which I hold as I write. I also hold it as I work my day job and wash my dishes, just as the baseball player holds his purpose as he waits in the dugout or warms up in the batter's box.

Boil your mission statement down to a specific, recognizable sense of purpose that is as natural and comfortable to you as the craftsman's is to him. But not too comfortable—don't worry if there's an edge to it. You want that purpose to cut through life as serenely as an icebreaker.

Be great

The way we do small things is a sign of how we would do bigger things. If you haven't yet achieved greatness in your life, take a look at how you treat the details.

Think of the construction of a house. Drawing up plans for a magnificent villa is all well and good, but it can't be expected to stand if care hasn't been taken to make each and every joint straight and secure.

Evolving into a master craftsman has a great deal to do with paying attention to all the corners, all the edges, all the wires. It has to do with not letting things slide, but rather taking infinite pains to perfect them—small things, like polished stones, level surfaces, perfectly stretched canvases.

Any time we slide into a negative state of mind, we're prone to sloppy craftsmanship. A sloppy craftsman will leave a finish rough or legs uneven. It's convenient to think that no one notices, but everyone does. If it doesn't hit the viewer in the eye right off the bat, it detracts from the general sense of quality, and don't kid yourself, people feel it. They may not know precisely why, but they will know something's not quite right. It's just a little cheap, they think. Better give it a miss.

If you fall into this trap at work, you'll lose your job for the wrong reasons. Instead, make sure you complete all your tasks with an air of greatness. Do everything as well it can be done or better, even if you're the only one who notices.

The tasks we don't enjoy require the most attention, just to be sure. Accept the challenge of doing the vilest or most boring jobs with style. Be a master craftsman all the way to the bottom of the pile.

A detail can be as simple as the arrangement of objects on your desk, which affects the rest of the office staff as much as it affects you and your ability to do your work well. It can be your conscientiousness in finishing off every last bit of the job at hand. You might decide to make a change in the way you contribute to teamwork or bring a new, lighter attitude to the atmosphere, perhaps by not placing responsibility on everyone else or by letting a criticism go, even when it wasn't your fault. The change doesn't have to be big. It can be a subtle, almost imperceptible shift from reluctance to willingness. You can go the extra mile for your coworkers by doing additional filing or cleaning up the coffee station.

There's a kind of magic in this approach. As you pay attention to the smallest tasks, making sure you do them as thoroughly and beautifully as you can, your surroundings become more pleasant to be in, which is a great thing, and you yourself become correspondingly great. The greater you get, the smaller your job becomes.

Being great means never being too big to do the small things, and to do them well.

Thoughts and actions for
Be great

1. Generate care for what you do.

It's possible to generate care, and even love, for something simply by intending to do so. Intend to love your work, and even if you miss the mark, you'll still feel better about it. Intend to care about every action simply because you're doing it.

Slow down and watch yourself do things. Are you doing them with care? If you're doing a task at work that you don't really care about, ask yourself how you'd do it if it were for you, if you loved it, then do it that way. Make sure everything you do is done with an air of quiet greatness, from cleaning the toilet to filing your taxes.

A quarryman was asked how he could possibly sing under such wretched conditions while everyone around him was groaning in pain. "I'm not toiling in a quarry," he said. "I'm building a cathedral."

2. Make it beautiful.

Give the same quality of aesthetic care to tasks at work that you give to your art. Type a letter as if it were your unpublished novel. Make your bed as if you were arranging a quilt for show.

Everything you do is an extension of you. You really are the work of art. Let it show! Place the stamp on the envelope in just the right place, bring a beautiful mug to work in place of a paper cup, or introduce a color-coded system that will simplify filing for your coworkers.

Art isn't just about aesthetics, of course. Openness, amazement, curiosity, focus, intent—all that and more is what making art is about. Whatever your artistic temperament may be, bring it to work and apply it to the most mundane tasks. Be an artist through and through.

Increase and abound

Have you ever noticed how much time we spend keeping our environment from overgrowing? We're constantly whacking down tree-high weeds from our yards and hauling off mountains of clutter from our offices, not to mention what-was-I-thinking novelty yarn and prehistoric dried-out paint tubes from our workshops. Everything on this planet yearns toward increase and abundance, and we often have a hard time staying on top of it all.

We go to great lengths to keep things in order. We invent lawn-mowing machines we can ride on, set up enormous and complex filing systems, and erect entire buildings just to hold our stuff.

Abundance and increase is clearly in the nature of life. Our desire to create more abundant, fulfilling futures is as natural to us as bearing acorns is to an oak tree. Embrace this wonderful aspect of yourself—especially at your day job, where you need it the most.

This is what Wattles has to say about it:

"Whether you change your vocation or not, you must direct your present actions to the business in which you are presently engaged.

"You can get into the business you want by making constructive use of the business you are already in. . . . And insofar as your business consists in dealing with other people—whether directly, by telephone, or by letter—the key thought of all your efforts must be to convey to their minds the impression of increase."

Why? Because, he says, "Increase is what all men and women are seeking. It is the urge of the formless intelligence within them to find fuller expression."

This urge is what drives you to want to create in the first place. Your desire to express yourself in art is this formless intelligence within you seeking expression. It's what gave form to the oak trees and it's what gave form to you.

It's not surprising if you find yourself dissatisfied with a mindless job or working for peanuts. The life force always wants more and greater things for itself. If you acknowledge this desire for increase and abundance in your own life, it will help you move from where you are to a place closer to where you want to be.

Because the entire planet is seeking increase, people are naturally attracted to those individuals who convey it. Be aware of this aspect of your nature and let it convey itself to others. You don't need to advertise—in fact, you don't need to say anything about it at all. Just hold the faith that you are an increasing and abundant person in an increasing and abundant universe. People will respond, and opportunities will come your way.

Think about the people you know. Is there anyone in your acquaintance who conveys a quiet sense of abundance? Ask yourself how you respond to this. If you find yourself responding in a negative way, you are actually pushing away your own prosperity.

How might this look in the life of a painter? He starts squirming a little within his own work, dreaming of larger spaces. He lets his canvases grow and before long, he's draping trees with color and writing his name in the sky. People begin to say, "Oh yes, that's the guy who paints the sides of skyscrapers. Amazing stuff!" They start calling him for huge commissions, the really big ones no one else can handle. Soon, he's too big to ever fit back in his box. He let himself grow.

Not everyone's dream is this big, but maybe you do want to be bigger than your own box. As Wattles writes: "You are a creative center from which increase is given off to all."

Thoughts and actions for
Increase and abound

1. Create, don't compete.

As you cultivate an awareness of increase and abundance in your life, remember that you are not competing with anyone else. There's no need to. Each of us is a creative center. There is no lack in the universe. No one can take from you what is rightfully yours.

In your mind, plug into the growth that is all around you. Think of the sprouting plants, the ever-renewing waterfalls, the jungles of the Amazon. Know that nature never stops abounding. I experienced a brushfire once that almost took my house. The scorched earth reached six feet from the door of my workshop, which was filled with wooden looms. For months afterward, my village was surrounded by blackened dirt and the smell of charcoal and ash. Then one day, without rain, the leaves and the grass started pushing through again. Soon, the trees and fields were green.

Let the energy of renewable increase infuse your life. Channel it outward, and remember that there's more where that came from.

2. Declutter.

Let's take a look at the other end of the spectrum and tackle the increase we can't seem to stop. Try nourishing only the sort of increase you want by avoiding the masses of "stuff" that tend to pile up around you. The more unused stuff that fills your life, the less you'll have of the stuff you really want.

Declutter often. Keep your environment clear of excess baggage. Flylady, a well-known clutter expert, proposes jumping up periodically and spending 15 minutes tossing into a garbage bag the first 27 unnecessary things you see in your immediate vicinity. This is a wonderful exercise she calls "The 27-Fling Boogie." The trick is not to belabor it. Don't lovingly ponder each item, just keep moving. If it hits you as junk, it's junk.

Pruning your clutter on a regular basis will keep you focused on your goal. Only keep around you what you're working on or working toward. Do you need it? Do you love it? No? Get rid of it.

You can see this decluttering process in nature as well. The fire in my village might have scared the daylights out of us, but it also cleared out choking underbrush and dying trees. Declutter your own life before nature does it for you.

Advance

A plant can increase dramatically in size over the course of a season without having advanced. Advancement is a concept that implies transcendent growth, the kind of growth that leads to leaps in technology or the invention of a new medium. It's not just moving, but moving forward into a qualitatively better place.

What I'm suggesting here, in our case, is cosmic career placement. Think of it this way: promotion is not something only your boss can do for you. You can take your own situation in hand and promote yourself to a new position.

There are exactly two people on the staff of the small-town weekly newspaper where I work. Our publisher, the owner of the business, is located in a nearby town where he puts out another weekly newspaper. I know that I could work my heart out, which I do, for the rest of my life and there will never be a promotion for me on this paper the way it is. There's simply no position available. I work here for a variety of reasons, but I do acknowledge that it's my choice. Given the circumstances, and given my belief that I deserve a better position even though there isn't one to be had, I decided the best thing to do was to give myself a promotion.

It's good to have a specialty, and newspaper reporting has sharpened my skills and given me something to grab onto. But in the larger scheme of things, in terms of cosmic career placement, I'm a writer, and I count reporting among my skills. This advances me in my own mind and opens me up to unexpected marketable opportunities. As I was making plans to move back to Europe, I gave myself a promotion to language consultant and drew up a business plan to sell my services to small companies in Zurich. When my plans changed and I decided to stay here instead, I started a business that produces letterpress and other printed items, so now I'm a business owner and artist as well.

As a result, I've given myself more opportunities as well as greater esteem. I accept that I'm bigger than my job. I envision myself advancing and am watching myself advance. When the time is right, I'll step out of my present position and into the new one.

Your advancement might be to another job within your existing company, or it might be to a company you didn't know existed, or to the wonderful world of freelancing. It might be completely out of your present field and into something you couldn't have predicted. Whatever it is, make it a promotion you bestow upon yourself by claiming it within your own mind. Don't leave it to the chance of a rubber stamp.

Keep the idea of your own advancement in your mind at all times. Hold to your vision, act with purpose, align your thoughts with your goal, and do your day completely. Give heartfelt thanks for all your blessings. You are not restricted to only the possibilities you see in front of you. In fact, if you head into only what you can see, you'll be getting more of the same, forever.

Will you be able to direct the course of your advancement at all times? I can't see how that's possible, as we're never doing it alone. Although you may know where you want to go, the path will hold surprising twists, and it will certainly veer off into territory you weren't expecting. Roll with it. Opportunities will come your way, ideas will occur to you, doors will open, old friends and new acquaintances will appear, and the next steps will become clearer every day.

You'll know when the time is right to make a change. In the meantime, may God bless you right where you are.

The Crazy Quilt of Life

A little bit about me

Ten years ago, in one of my countless day-job incarnations, I was plugging away at a mind-numbing translation when I had the idea to make a list of all the ways that I keep myself awake and sane on the job.

That was the birth of an article called "11 Tips for Surviving a Day Job With Your Sanity Intact." I sent the article to Chris Dunmire, owner of the website creativity-portal.com, and one week later, it had gone viral. I heard from people as far away as a professor in New Zealand, who asked if he could reprint it in his textbook.

It occurred to me that there was a need for this information, and I started writing *Day Job Survival Kit*. It took me ten years to get this far.

I tell you this to give you heart. Don't give up.

It's true that my graduate studies were in psychology of art, that I studied studio arts for years, am a creativity coach trained by Eric Maisel, and that I've been living with the principles in this book for many years. But what amazes me is the trail of day jobs I've left behind.

In the years leading up to my "11 Tips" article, I'd served my dues as a waitress, a barmaid, a sandwich maker in a sidewalk stand, a babysitter, and a homecare worker for the elderly. I'd worked in a nursing home, a couple of offices, and an oil refinery. Let's not forget my first real job, while still a high school student, at a trophy-engraving shop, where I swept floors and ruined my fair share of metal plaques, followed by a stint at Macy's flagship store in Manhattan after graduation.

When I went back to college in my 30s, I supplemented my student loans and grants with jobs in the school's maintenance department and re-entry office. I graded papers for my English teacher, read timed texts for court-reporting students at a business college, cleaned the local YWCA, and worked perhaps my favorite day job of all: bagel bagger at the Grateful Bagel, in Santa Rosa, California.

At college, I studied painting. My intention was to teach somewhere in the art field at the college level. Yes, I actually believed I could have a career. Instead, I took my MA and moved to Europe, where I lived for many years. My degree and my English (along with my Swiss passport) got me a succession of interesting jobs, just not the one I was trained to do.

I started out teaching English in language schools and then spent a year or so in the archives of the architectural university in Zurich. Following that was a position as the publications manager for a student travel confederation before the office moved to Copenhagen without me and I found a job assisting the legal staff in the claims department of the second-largest reinsurance company in the world.

At that point, I was convinced that I had drifted as far as possible from my original dream of teaching and practicing the arts. I cried myself to sleep more often than not, and as I look back on it now, I see how blind I was to the blessings I'd been given.

But life took a surprising turn when I had back problems that took me away from that job. My solution was to learn to translate German into English and work at home, which I did and still do. That freelance work allowed me to move from Switzerland to the Mediterranean island of Corsica, where I stayed for five years, created a weaving atelier, and put my creativity coach training to work.

My winding path, however, took me to Vermont, where I worked as a hostess at a country inn, back to Europe one more time, on to Mexico, and here to Missouri, where I've been living for the last five years with my furry feline companion, Lucy, and working my current day job as a reporter for the town newspaper. But you never know what life has in store, and I'm thinking it just might be time to move again.

Throughout all this day-job kerfuffle, I've managed to write the drafts for two books along with numerous articles on the creative process. My life has stayed colorful with textiles, beading, painting, and writing, and as we speak, I'm plotting my move into letterpress and book arts. I'm also building a freelance writing business in addition to the translating, with the goal of working completely from home once again.

If there is one word that describes the landscape of my professional and creative lives, it would have to be "patchwork." It's been a crazy quilt, and I've finally come to embrace it.

The moral of this story, as far as I can see, is that there's always a way to be happy. Stay positive, stay creative, and keep your eye on the goal. I have been blessed with the greatest spiritual guidance I could ever have hoped for. If you aren't praying regularly as yet, start. Know what you want and ask for God's help.

May He bless you always,
Durga Walker

Connect with Me

Come visit my brand-new baby website, The Artful Day Jobber, at www.dayjobsurvival.com. DJS has plans to grow into a very helpful site, with resources, success stories, and lots and lots of encouragement. Leave your email address for notification of future products and developments, and I promise I will never attack you with spam. However, I *might* ask you to buy a "Day Job Survivor" t-shirt—you never know.

Many Thanks!

If you enjoyed reading *The Day Job Survival Kit*, please leave a review at Amazon.com. Reviews are helpful to other readers, but they are also helpful to authors. Tell me what you liked and what you didn't like. Help me make the next book better. Thank you for reading and for your feedback!

About the Author

Photo by Cassi Friend

Durga Walker is living proof that day jobs need not stand in the way of creative dreams. Day-jobber by day and artist by night, Durga first wrote *The Day Job Survival Kit* as a web article entitled "11 Tips for Surviving a Day Job With Your Sanity Intact." The article and the book were both born from the nightmare faced by all creative souls holding down jobs they don't love. Durga has relocated around the world almost as much as she's changed jobs. She currently lives in Missouri, where by day she's a reporter on a small-town newspaper. By night and weekend, she writes, paints, and builds a freelance business. Durga has an M.A. in communication arts and training in creativity coaching.

Made in the USA
Lexington, KY
16 December 2016